Is Technology Good for Education?

Is Technology Good for Education?

NEIL SELWYN

polity

The right of Neil Selwyn to be identified as Author of this Work has been asserted in accordance with the UK Copyright, Designs and Patents Act 1988.

First published in 2016 by Polity Press

Polity Press
65 Bridge Street
Cambridge CB2 1UR, UK

Polity Press
350 Main Street
Malden, MA 02148, USA

ISBN-13: 978-0-7456-9646-1
ISBN-13: 978-0-7456-9647-8 (pb)

Library of Congress Cataloging-in-Publication Data

Names: Selwyn, Neil, author.
Title: Is technology good for education? / Neil Selwyn.
Description: Cambridge, UK : Malden, MA : Polity Press, [2016] | Includes
  bibliographical references.
Identifiers: LCCN 2015034951| ISBN 9780745696461 (hardback : alk. paper) |
  ISBN 9780745696478 (pbk. : alk. paper)
Subjects: LCSH: Education--Effect of technological innovations on. |
  Educational technology--Evaluation. | Computer-assisted
  instruction--Evaluation. | Education--Aims and objectives.
Classification: LCC LB1028.3 .S388857 2016 | DDC 371.33--dc23 LC record available
at http://lccn.loc.gov/2015034951

A catalogue record for this book is available from the British Library.

Typeset in 11 on 15 Adobe Garamond by
Servis Filmsetting Ltd, Stockport, Cheshire
Printed and bound in the United Kingdom by Clays Ltd, St Ives PLC

For further information on Polity, visit our website: politybooks.com

CONTENTS

Preface　　　　　　　　　　　　　　　　　　vi

1　Digital Technology and Educational Change　　1

2　Making Education More Democratic?　　26

3　Making Education More Personalized?　　54

4　Making Education More Calculable?　　81

5　Making Education More Commercial?　　107

6　'Good' Education and the Digital – So What
　　Needs to Change?　　133

Notes　　161
Index　　176

As many readers will have guessed already, the answer to this book's title is 'yes/no/all points in between'. The confluence of technology and education is complicated, contradictory and messy. There are no easy answers and no clear solutions. On one hand, titles that start from the premise of 'Is Technology Good For . . . ?' can be criticized justifiably as 'stupefyingly dualistic' and indicative of the 'simplification' that has eroded recent public discussion over digital futures.[i] On the other hand, these continue to be the types of question that many people find themselves asking on a daily basis. This book therefore adopts what might be seen as a rather crude premise as the starting point from which to explore a range of difficult issues and debates that are *not* usually part of the 'ed-tech' debate. This is a book intended to make you think otherwise about technology and education.

[i] Astra Taylor and Joanne McNeil (2014) 'The dads of tech', *The Baffler*, 26 (www.thebaffler.com/salvos/dads-tech).

'This is a book
intended to make
you think otherwise
about technology and
education.'

A main ambition for writers working in the social sciences and humanities is to produce 'apt characterizations' of important topics that otherwise tend to be described inadequately in popular and political circles.[ii] In this spirit, the underlying intention of this book is to develop an apt characterization of technology and education: that is, to present the key issues and debates relating to 'ed-tech' in appropriately nuanced and aware ways. This book therefore seeks to shift the nature of the conversation about technology and education. It does not set out to make spectacular predictions or present hitherto unseen evidence. Instead it offers an opportunity to pause for thought and to take stock. In an area of digital society that is infused with hyperbole and exaggeration, such an interruption is surely a 'good' thing.

That said, this is a book that takes the 'hype' of education and technology seriously. In the spirit of Polity's 'Digital Futures' series, the following six chapters focus deliberately on the 'freshest contemporary aspects of the current literature' and 'ideas that are shaking up the field at the moment'. So veteran observers of education and/or technology should be warned from the outset that this book

[ii] Stefan Collini (2013) *What are universities for?* London: Penguin.

does contain prolonged discussions of topics such as the 'disruption' of education, digital 'personalization' and other such buzzwords. There may well be some readers who feel immediately contemptuous of such debates. Indeed, much of the talk that surrounds technology and education certainly mimics the generally vacuous and enthusiastic excesses of 'tech-talk'. For some critics, then, it is tempting to see these ideas and agendas as simply not worthy of serious attention.

Yet while reacting to these current ideas and debates as little more than nonsense, noise and hype is understandable (especially from an academic perspective), these are arguments that should not be simply ignored and dismissed out of hand. Whether we like it or not, these are all arguments that are being taken very seriously by policy-makers, industrialists and many other powerful groups *outside* of education. These are ideas about educational futures that currently are directing billions of dollars of investment. Conversely, these are also arguments that many people *inside* education are not fully engaged with, yet are already beginning to feel the effects of. As such, this book aims to give these ideas and assumptions a fair hearing while also looking to develop more credible alternatives. Whatever your position on the past, present and future of education, these are arguments that require attention.

So, before we get started, I would like to thank Andrea Drugan at Polity for pitching this as one of the initial titles in the 'Digital Futures' series, and Elen Griffiths for her subsequent work in getting the book published. Thanks to Justin Dyer for copy-editing the final draft. I would also like to thank Scott Bulfin, Luci Pangrazio and Selena Nemorin for their ongoing conversations about technology, education and society throughout the writing of this book. My writing on the topic has definitely been much improved by their support.

Neil Selwyn
Melbourne
October 2015

ONE

Digital Technology and Educational Change

Introduction

Digital technology is now an integral part of education. The past forty years have seen exponential increases in computer processing power accompanied by major technological developments such as the internet and mobile telephony. Smartphones, tablets and other computerized devices are now common means of interacting with people, consuming media, engaging with the core institutions in our societies and generally living out many aspects of everyday life. Google and Wikipedia are the first places that millions of people turn to when wanting to access information and find things out. These technologies alone have transformed the generation and communication of knowledge and, it follows, the ways in which learning and understanding take place. In all these ways, many important elements of education are now profoundly digital.

Of course, 'education' extends far beyond matters of learning and engaging with knowledge. In an organizational sense, digital technologies are now central to the 'formal' organization and governance of compulsory and post-compulsory education. Schools, colleges and universities operate along increasingly digital lines, while alternate forms of online education have emerged to complement and/ or compete with traditional 'bricks and mortar' institutions. Hundreds of millions of people are enrolled in online courses and other forms of virtual study. Billions of dollars are spent every year by state and federal governments on digital educational resources. National educational technology policies and initiatives are launched regularly by governments around the world, all striving to keep up with the demands of the digital age. What shall be referred to throughout this book as 'digital education' is entwined with matters of global economics and politics, as well as ongoing changes in what 'counts' as knowledge, skills and learning. All told, digital technology is an increasingly integral element of 'education' in the broadest sense.

On a day-to-day basis, however, the digital tends to be experienced as routine and unremarkable. Digital technologies are simply part of the way that we now 'do' education, as well as how education is 'done' to us. For many people, digital technologies

'To what extent is digital technology *really* changing education – and is this *always* in our best interests?'

have become a background feature of everyday education. Yet it is unwise to be blasé about the presence of digital technology in education settings. Beyond the immediate 'education community' of teachers, students, technology developers and other involved professionals, it is telling that policy-makers, industrialists and other influential actors usually frame digital technologies in education in dramatic terms of wide-scale change and reform. So rather than getting bogged down in prosaic discussions of how specific digital devices or applications might be used more effectively by teachers or schools, many people *outside* of education are keen to speculate in more ambitious terms. For instance, might digital technology do away with the need for teachers and schools altogether? Why should thousands of universities be funded to deliver different versions of what are essentially the same courses when the best professors can be beamed repeatedly to anywhere in the world? From this perspective, digital technology presents a fundamental challenge to everything that we have come to know as 'education' over the past hundred years or so. This book focuses on the ways in which this potential for radical change might *actually* be realized. To what extent is digital technology *really* changing education – and is this *always* in our best interests?

Digital technology and education change

Most discussions about the uses of digital technologies in education are concerned with educational change. This is to be expected, as digital technologies tend to be associated with change across all areas of society. Very few people set out to use digital technology in order to do things in exactly the same ways as before. Instead, digital technologies are usually associated with doing things in cheaper, faster, more convenient, more exciting or more efficient ways. If not leading to changes for the better, then digital technologies tend to be implicated with detrimental change along the lines of 'Google making us stupid' or 'text messaging making kids less literate'. Either way, it is common sense to align digital technologies with change and things being different. Indeed, digital technologies are perhaps best understood as 'mediating' non-digital processes and practices: making some new things possible while at the same time introducing new limitations and unintended consequences.

The potential of digital technologies to change education tends to be imagined along a spectrum ranging from modest improvement to wholesale revolution. At one level, digital technologies are celebrated as leading to distinct *improvements* in education. Often this relates to improving learning (e.g. making learning more social, 'situated' or 'authentic') or improving learners (e.g. getting them engaged, motivated or able to learn). Descriptions recur of technology 'enhancing', 'enabling', 'assisting', 'supporting' and 'scaffolding' learning. In a similar vein, digital technologies are also welcomed as expanding the capacity of teachers to teach, heightening the efficiency of educational institutions and increasing the relevance of education systems to the needs of society and economy. All told, a sense emerges of education being improved and upgraded while remaining essentially the same in terms of its institutions, organization and general ways of doing things.

Another heightened level of change, however, sees digital technologies associated with the *transformation* of educational processes and practices. This refers to a marked renewal and 'shaking up' of the nature and form of 'education'. This shift in language implies a set of fundamental changes, such as courses being delivered online rather than face-to-face, people learning through playing games rather than being taught directly, and so on. Tellingly, these changes are sometimes described in language borrowed from the worlds of computer engineering and the IT industry. For example, the vernacular of software development is often used to indicate significant improvements in functionality. Thus we hear talk of 'School 2.0' and 'Education 3.0'. Continuing this theme, some commentators talk of 'upgrading', 'hacking' or 'rebooting' education. All of these descriptions imply a recoding and re-scripting of the rules of education. The purposes of education are being renewed, with digital technology acting as a catalyst and a facilitator of these changes.

More extreme still is the idea that digital technologies are leading to wholesale *revolution* in education – suggesting an overthrowing of the established order and vested interests. This severity of change is more pronounced than the straightforward idea of 'transformation', implying a contentious, violent and bloody form of change. Indeed, 'revolution' conveys a sense of conflict, clashes of interests and ideologies, the overthrowing of established elites, the challenging of the status quo and the redistribution of power and control. Some of the main targets of this upheaval are dominant institutions such as 'the school' and 'the university', formal examination and qualification systems, national curricula and suchlike. Digital technology is also seen to destabilize the 'education establishment' of teachers, unions and academics, as well as government agencies and state institutions.

In contrast, digital technology is framed as empowering previously marginalized groups: in particular, advancing the interests of individuals over institutions, parents over professionals, private markets over public sector monopolies and outsiders over insiders. With these kinds of technology-driven radical change, very little in education is expected ever to be the same again.

A digital 'fix' for a 'broken' system?

These changes tend to be discussed in confident and compelling ways. Thinking carefully about the language that is used to describe education and digital technology is a theme that recurs throughout this book. One of the most significant aspects of 'digital education' is its discursive nature. In other words, the values and meanings that are attached to the *idea* of digital education could be seen as just as significant as any actual use of digital technology. This certainly chimes with the ways in which digital education often is experienced 'on the ground'. There has been, for example, little rigorous evidence produced over the past forty years of technology leading to the sustained improvement of teaching and learning. Similarly, most education institutions and systems certainly do not appear to be in the throes of full-scale revolt or even partial transformation. Much of the rhetoric of digital education has proven frustratingly difficult to substantiate.

We are perhaps better off treating these descriptions of digital 'revolution', 'transformation' and 'improvement' as evocative and aspirational stories, rather than sober, objective and accurate descriptions of actual ongoing changes in education. The primary significance of these stories is what they tell us about wider hopes, fears, desires and expectations surrounding contemporary education – particularly in fast-changing technological, economic, political and demographic times. 'Digital education' is a potent space for voicing hopes and fears of what education might become in the near future. We would do well, therefore, to treat any overly confident assertions of digital change in a circumspect and sceptical manner.

In this spirit, it is worth paying attention to the prominent argument that digital technology is a ready 'fix' for education systems that are outmoded, no longer fit for purpose and generally 'broken'. Over the past decade or so, the idea of technological 'disruption' of outmoded industries and business models has become one of the most familiar – and overused – ways to describe digital innovation. The internet, for example, is now presumed to be having a far-reaching disruptive effect on many areas of society, from the newspaper industry to high street retailing. It certainly seems reasonable to question how much longer people will be prepared to pay for daily newspapers that are printed on paper and sold from news-stands. It is also reasonable to question people's continued willingness to traipse to stores in the hope of purchasing goods that they then are expected to transport home. These are generally accepted to be 'traditional' industries and markets in the midst of substantial upheaval.

For many people, the idea of digital renewal is equally applicable to education. *The Economist* magazine recently turned its attention towards the 'reinvention of the university' and concluded bluntly: 'The internet, which has turned businesses from newspapers through music to book retailing upside down, will upend higher education.'[1] Similarly, as media commentator Jeff Jarvis has proclaimed, '[E]ducation is one of the institutions most deserving of disruption – and with the greatest opportunities to come of it.'[2] To the unfamiliar eye these can come across as highly provocative propositions. These statements constitute a direct challenge to the institutionalization of education – most notably in the form of universities and schools, as well as state-run education systems and the bureaucratic agencies and organizations that surround them.

The Economist and Jarvis are by no means alone in voicing this concern. It is now common to hear mention of education as being 'broken', or an outmoded and obsolete product of a bygone era. People speak with exasperation of the 'industrial era classroom', the 'factory model' school, 'ivory tower' universities, and so on. Such descriptions are intended to convey a sense of the mismanagement of education by monolithic institutions that are profoundly undemocratic and archaic. These are lumbering organizations where ownership, control and power are concentrated unfairly in the hands of elites – be they vice chancellors and university professors, or school district superintendents, tenured teachers and their unions. Like many large administrations and bureaucracies, these are institutions that are believed to be unresponsive, incompetent, untrustworthy, ungrateful, self-serving and greedy.[3] As such, these are institutions that clearly 'deserve' to be swept away.

Such arguments have understandably caught the attention of many people outside of education (as well as a fair number of people on the inside). As Martin Weller contends, the notion that 'education is broken' has 'become such an accepted standpoint that it is often stated as an irrefutable fact. . . . It is simply stated as a starting position, from which all else follows, a *sine qua non* of educational revolution.'[4] At a push, such claims are sometimes specified in terms of a perceived lack of creativity in teaching approaches and curriculum content, entrenched problems with truancy rates, the so-called 'school to prison pipeline' and/or the financial unsustainability of higher education. Yet, regardless of these details, such prognoses tend to be advanced by interests outside of education wishing to promote alternative forms of education. This encompasses groups seeking the reform of education from the various perspectives of the free market, libertarianism, home-schooling, child-centred learning, and so on. While the motivations for making such claims might differ considerably, the logic is usually one of justifying some form of external intervention. As Weller observes, these are 'manipulative' accounts that imply that educators and education professionals cannot continue to be trusted. Instead, the presumed solution is for external agents to be allowed to make sweeping changes: 'If something is diagnosed as broken, then the appropriate response is to fix it. The search then becomes for a solution, and very often those people who are determining education to be broken, also stand to profit from providing an alternative solution.'[5]

In many ways, such criticisms are difficult to wholly refute. The case can be easily made that the dominant educational institutions in our lives are 'broken'. Let us take the recent plight of US education as one example.[6] Here, despite spending more than most other countries on its schools (over $10,000 on each student per year), the United States languishes in the bottom half of international indictors when it comes to mathematics, science and reading ability. In addition to these indicators of stuttering learning quality, US schools can be criticized for their basic failure to see students through the system. Schools in the United States are notoriously porous. With an annual drop-out rate of 1.2 million students, the statistic is often cited of 7,000 students dropping out of US high schools for every day of the year (or one student for every twenty-six seconds). All told, it is reckoned that around one quarter of high school freshmen fail to graduate on time. Recently, much concern has been expressed over the 1,500 or so high schools across the country labelled as 'drop-out factories': that is, graduating less than 60 per cent of their students. Clearly not all schools are perfect, even in the world's most advanced economies.

The situation is no better in post-compulsory education.[7] On one hand, the United States spends more on higher education as a percentage of gross domestic product than almost any other nation: 2.6 per cent as opposed to 1.6 per cent in Australia and 1.3 per cent in the United Kingdom and Germany. On the other hand, drop-out rates are higher than in most other countries. Nearly half of US college students fail to graduate with a degree after six years at college or university. The privilege of university study burdens students with increasing levels of debt and ever-dwindling prospects of 'graduate'-level employment. When presented in these terms, the product being offered by most universities is difficult to justify. As David Bromwich reflects:

> [T]he price of a college education [is] so high that today on average it costs eleven times as much as it did in 1978. Underlying the anxiety about the worth of a college degree is a suspicion that old methods and the old knowledge will soon be eclipsed by technology. . . . A potent fear is that all but a few colleges and universities will soon be driven out of business.[8]

So, rather than patching up the same old institutions, systems and structures that we have always had, digital technology is associated increasingly with radical forms of educational innovation and upheaval. For many commentators, digital technologies are a means of shaking things up, sweeping away old regimes and reimagining and remaking education provision in forms fit for the twenty-first century. This may well sound like the type of extreme talk that appeals only to a radical fringe, but statements about digital 'disruption', 'revolution' and 'reinvention' are now beginning to pass into educational common sense. Yet as with all forms of common sense, rather than accepting these stories at face value, we would do well to take time to consider what is actually being argued for here. These are big ideas with big implications.

'Disruptive innovation' and the digital fixing of education

It is useful to trace these popular sentiments about technology and education back to their origins in economics and business thinking. While it is not often mentioned by name, much of the recent educational talk about the disruption of education stems back to the writing of Clay Christensen on 'disruptive innovation'. This describes the phenomenon of low-spec and relatively ordinary technologies being used to address emerging values, needs and desires not being catered for elsewhere. Often these simple applications and ideas might seem counter-intuitive or inferior in comparison to the current dominant, successful ways of doing things. Nevertheless, these disruptive innovations thrive on the basis of being able to successfully make products and services available to new populations previously not able to access them. Over time these niche ways of doing things with new populations take root and eventually expand into the established marketplace. This will then lower prices and force existing providers to change their ways or else go out of business.

More often than not, Christensen contends, well-established institutions will ignore new innovation as long as it falls outside of their existing 'value networks': that is, what is required to continue to compete successfully against current competitors. Instead, these institutions will focus most attention on what he calls 'sustaining innovations': things that have helped them historically succeed and sustain the attributes that have grown to be most valued in their market. Big organizations are understandably most interested in innovations that allow them to get 'incrementally bigger, more powerful and more efficient'[9] at the things that they already do. In the meantime, new innovators such as small 'start-up' firms and entrepreneurs will emerge – all able and willing to inhabit different value networks and cater for 'non-consumers' who could not otherwise access traditional forms of the service. Every so often, one of these alternative ways of doing things will expand until the point that they can invade and 'disrupt' the existing established marketplace. As Christensen puts it, 'Eventually the quality becomes just good enough for the established customers to flock to it.'[10] At this point, the new market and new value network become the norm, and the best that older institutions can do is attempt to play catch-up. Then, the disruption is complete.

A much-cited example of disruptive innovation in the digital age has been the impact of Wikipedia on the encyclopaedia business. Who could have predicted that the market for information reference books could be reshaped around values of community authorship, the wisdom of crowds rather than the word of individual experts, constantly changing content, online publishing rather than bound volumes, and all produced on a non-profit basis? More pointedly, who could have foreseen that after 2010 *Encyclopaedia Britannica* would cease to publish a print edition? Why, then, should education be any different?

The appeal of the digital fix

Many people anticipate the digital disruption of education over the next ten years or so along similar lines to the printed encyclopaedia business. One can certainly see why this might be a welcome proposition. First, there is much to be disgruntled about when it comes to the current state of education. Clearly, school and university systems are not 'working' as well as they might. Similarly, many students, teachers, parents and employers are undoubtedly being let down by their education systems. It would certainly seem that a strong case exists for rethinking education from the ground upwards. As Todd Hixon argued with regard to the US university system:

> Higher Ed has a product that does not work, ridiculous costs, and an antiquated business model. For many years we accepted this because we see extraordinary value in education. Now, most middle and upper-middle class parents find they cannot give their children the education they enjoyed. Technology has recently put a spark to this fuel: on-line education works and dramatically improves costs and access. This is a big opportunity for entrepreneurs and investors.[11]

Second, the disruption thesis certainly goes a long way towards explaining the long-standing 'no show' of much educational technology innovation from the 1970s to the present day. As was implied earlier, one of the great conundrums of educational technology over the past forty years or so has been its relative lack of impact. Of course, technology-related changes to education have abounded at a superficial level. Yet for the most part, the essence of education has remained the same: punctuated by an entrenched 'grammar' of doing things that reinforces the notion of the expert 'teacher' and the regulation of time, space and place, alongside the routines of curriculum and pedagogy, and rituals of assessment and credentializing. Throughout this time it has been difficult to look beyond the diagnosis offered by educational historian Larry Cuban at the beginning of the 1990s when he observed bluntly that 'computer meets classroom, classroom wins'.[12] Looking at the persistence of the school classroom set-up with the teacher positioned front-of-stage, or the continued reliance in most universities on the large-scale lecture, it is easy to see why people frequently still feel driven to trot out variations on the cliché that 'the classroom of today has changed little from the classroom of one hundred years ago'.

The disruptive innovation thesis offers a neat way around this inconvenient truth of the 'no significant difference' of educational technology. The idea of disruptive innovation offers the justification that most of these previous efforts were 'sustaining innovations' that stood little chance of altering the fundamental inefficiencies of the educational status quo. In contrast, the notion of digital disruption offers a new way of thinking about education and technology-driven change. Genuine disruption involves rethinking the very nature of education: its activities and relationships, as well as its core purposes and values. Genuine disruption is not about using technology to do the same things differently, but using technology to do fundamentally different things. This might involve engaging previously uninvolved or excluded people in educational activities, offering different products and services, striving for different outcomes, opening up new markets and finding new value. Genuine disruption requires interest groups and innovators from outside of the educational establishment to get involved in education provision. To evoke another common buzzword of recent times, digital technology is now finally beginning to act as a 'game changer'.

The inevitable digital change of education – reasons to be cautious

These are understandably exciting claims, yet they are best approached with caution and even suspicion. Surely such changes cannot be totally inevitable or wholly beneficial? At this point we need to look past the blind spot that many people appear to have developed when it comes to technology and education. Instead we need to think more carefully and critically about education and the digital. As such, we need to acknowledge a number of home truths to take forward into subsequent chapters of this book.

First and foremost, we need to recognize that all these claims of 'fixing', 'disrupting' and 'game changing' are being made for a reason. These are not value-free extrapolations of neutral technological innovation. Instead, any confident claim of imminent digital change is usually linked to wider agendas, beliefs and interests about education reform and broader societal change. Second – and to sharpen the focus of this initial observation – we need to recognize the corporate, commercial and economically driven nature of much of the prevailing talk of disruption and deinstitutionalization. The presence of corporate interests and commercial values in education is not necessarily a bad thing. Yet history suggests that business ideals, market values and the pursuit of profit often do not translate smoothly into education.

Third, history also reminds us that nothing is certain when it comes to technological change. From tackling drug addiction through to reducing highway accidents, there is rarely a neat, quick 'technical fix' for any societal problem.[13] This is particularly the case with education. Larry Cuban neatly demonstrated this in his book *Teachers and Machines*, which provided an expert review of the classroom failure of twentieth-century 'killer apps'. From the filmstrip of the 1910s through to educational radio of the 1930s and instructional television of the 1960s, the much-anticipated 'impact' of these technologies was almost always the same. Cuban details a 'strikingly uniform pattern of occasional teacher use' with the 'best ideas somehow los[ing] their vitality', resulting only in an 'anemic version of the original dream'.[14] While many educational changes arose from the use of these technologies, these were often not the changes that reformers and policy-makers were hoping for.

Finally, we need to remember that neither technological change nor educational change is a matter of 'common sense'. Indeed, alarm bells should start to ring as soon as anything is presented as being inevitable. Technological change is a complex process, and education is nowhere near as straightforward as these discourses of disruption would suggest. Any digital 'solution' in education is almost always accompanied by a number of unintended consequences, secondary effects and longer-term shifts. These are all issues that require much more scrutiny and critique.

Conclusions

This chapter has developed two broad contentions. First, digital education is undeniably a 'big deal'. Substantial changes are afoot that no-one in education can afford to ignore. Second, however, is the need to remain as dispassionate and circumspect as possible, and set about asking suitably critical questions. Despite all the chatter and noise to the contrary, this is an area where few things are certain and where there rarely are simple answers or predetermined narratives waiting to unfold. The ideas of digital improvement/transformation/disruption of education clearly require problematizing: that is, taking a step back from them and not taking them at face value. From now onwards we need to be inherently sceptical of the claims made about technology and education. This involves asking difficult questions of how digital technologies are *actually* finding a place in educational settings and educational contexts.

As Sonia Livingstone puts it, problematizing the place of technology in education involves three basic lines of inquiry: What is really going on? How can this be explained? How could things be otherwise?[15] Continuing in the spirit of asking straightforward but challenging questions of technology and education, we might want to add some more specific concerns:

- What is actually new here?
- What are the unintended consequences or second-order effects?
- What are the potential gains? What are the potential losses?
- What underlying values and agendas are implicit?
- In whose interests does this work? Who benefits in what ways?
- What are the social problems that digital technology is being presented as a solution to?
- How responsive to a 'digital fix' are these problems likely to be?

As the remainder of this book goes on to demonstrate, questions such as these make for insightful and involved discussions of the implications that digital technologies actually have for education. If we genuinely are concerned with improving education in the near future, then we now need to start asking these questions in earnest.

TWO

Making Education More Democratic?

Introduction

It could be argued that a prominent 'good' of digital technology lies in its capacity to support forms of education that are democratic and fair. This has certainly been a high-profile argument over the past few decades, not least from politicians looking to boost their reputations as socially concerned modernizers. During the 1990s, for instance, Bill Clinton was keen to tout computers as 'the great equalizer' in US schools.[1] Twenty years later, Barack Obama framed classroom Wi-Fi, laptops and mobile devices as providing otherwise disadvantaged students 'with a short path to the middle class'.[2] Alongside such politicking, billions of dollars have been spent by foundations, charities and voluntary organizations on equity-related education technology projects. As the Bill & Melinda Gates Foundation boasts: 'we are targeting the best new ideas that hold the greatest promise for improving the odds. . . . The power of technology is its ability to connect people, foster collaboration, empower learners and teachers, and challenge the status quo.'[3] Few people, it would seem, speak against the democratizing potential of digital education.

In contrast, there is general consensus that 'traditional' forms of education are nowhere near as fair or democratic as they could be. Education systems around the world are blighted by stark disparities in terms of access, participation and outcomes. Even in prosperous countries, high schools continue to be segregated in terms of their student intakes and subsequent rates of exclusion and (non-)completion. Similarly, the so-called 'massification' of university systems seems to have done little to counter long-standing disparities in terms of who benefits most from undergraduate and postgraduate study. While greater numbers of people are now entering higher education than ever before, clear divisions persist in terms of the types of subject studied, institutions attended and quality of degrees gained. In short, the best predictors of graduate success continue to be whether someone is male, white and from a high-income background – much as has been the case throughout the history of higher education.

Educational access, participation and outcomes therefore remain divided stubbornly along a recurring set of social fault-lines. In the United States, for instance, students from lower-income backgrounds are particularly disadvantaged in terms of the education they receive and the benefits that later accrue. These disadvantages are compounded for African-Americans and Latino/as, alongside those living in states such as Arkansas, New Mexico and Washington, which have some of the nation's lowest graduation rates. These trends are by no means confined to the United States, with similar inequalities and injustices persistent throughout many national education systems. Such concerns are complicated further when one considers the basic educational inequalities that blight developing and industrializing regions. It should not be forgotten that over 50 million children of primary school age receive no schooling at all. All told, making education more democratic and fair is a pressing matter around the world.

Digital technologies offer a logical means of addressing such problems. Indeed, it could be argued that the development of digital technologies over the past forty years or so has been imbued with promises of empowering individuals and improving people's lives. One of the initial motivations for the development of the 'personal computer' was to bring computing (previously limited to wealthy organizations) 'within the reach of the average person'.[4]

'Just why should digital education be any more successful in overcoming educational inequality and disadvantage than previous interventions and reforms?'

Twenty years later, in the words of Tim Berners-Lee, the worldwide web was designed as 'a radically open, egalitarian and decentralized platform ... vital to democracy and now more critical to free expression than any other medium'.[5] So why should such ambitions not continue with regard to education as we approach the 2020s?

The fact that digital technology has been seized upon as a potential clean slate for education is wholly understandable. After all, there are plenty of ways in which digital technologies might support forms of education that are easily accessed and engaged in by all. There are plenty of reasons why individuals might benefit from digital education regardless of material circumstance, personal background or other 'real-world' disadvantage. Yet, as was reasoned in chapter 1, education change is not simply a matter of common sense and good intentions. Instead, we need to consider some difficult rejoinders. Just why should digital education be any more successful in overcoming educational inequality and disadvantage than previous interventions and reforms? Why should the latest digital technologies be capable of overcoming entrenched patterns of disparity and disadvantage? What it is that makes people believe that digital education will be different?

Claims for the digital democratization of education

As just described, the 'unfairnesses' of education take a variety of long-standing forms. These include *inequalities of access*: that is, the fact that not everyone gets to participate in the education that they desire, regardless of how able and willing they might be. Of course, many forms of education are distinguished by the fact that they cannot be accessed by everybody. Selection criteria and entry requirements are a key part of education provision, from kindergarten to graduate school. In addition, there are many barriers to accessing education besides practical limits of class size and/or expected levels of 'academic ability'. Education might be provided in forms that are inconvenient – or downright impossible – for particular groups of people to access. Accessing education might not be a realistic option owing to issues of cost, transport, time, cultural norms or social expectations. Conversely, educational opportunities might not be publicized widely.

Inequalities persist even for those people who do get to take part. In particular, experiences and outcomes of education differ considerably according to who someone is – what is often referred to as *inequalities of participation*. Much has been made, for example, of the different experiences of school and university education if one is female, black or Latino/a, physically disabled and/or working class. These inequalities are evident in the disproportionately small numbers of such students who take high-status subjects, get the highest results and top classifications and generally are seen to 'succeed' in their educational endeavours. Less obvious inequalities also persist in terms of subtle discriminations, injustices and inconsistencies that some students experience because of who they are. Education can be 'unfair' in a variety of pernicious ways.

In the minds of many people, digital technologies turn all these problems on their head. First and foremost, digital technology can offer easier and more plentiful access to education. For example, the internet is seen to have dramatically increased educational choice and diversity over the past twenty years. The online provision of classes, courses and even entire school programmes has broadened the range of learning options available to people regardless of their immediate circumstances. The continually expanding provision of online courses and other modes of e-learning now provides even the most isolated individual with the opportunity of taking a course provided by Harvard or studying a niche topic such as Sanskrit. Alternately, people have the option to simply go online and teach themselves, or else learn with groups of other like-minded individuals. Education has long been considered a conversational, communal and collaborative process. Digital technologies are seen to be ideal spaces for such conversations and collaborations to take place.

Second, technology is also seen to offer more varied, more convenient and less costly means of participating in education. In this sense, digital technologies can act to reduce – or even remove – barriers to educational participation amongst previously excluded groups. In basic economic terms, digital technology allows for teaching and learning to be provided at considerably reduced financial cost than would otherwise be possible. In some cases, technology-based education can be offered for no cost at all. These shifts alone are seen to constitute a radically different way of allowing people to access education. As Kevin Carey argues: 'These historic developments will liberate hundreds of millions of people around the world, creating new ways of learning that have never existed before. They will also upend a cornerstone of the American meritocracy, fundamentally altering the way our society creates knowledge and economic opportunity.'[6]

Digitally based provision is also seen to reduce many of the 'situational' barriers that can prevent individuals taking part in education. These include family and other caring responsibilities, time and travel restrictions, physical effects of ageing or disability, employment constraints, and so on. More subtly, digital technologies might also reduce many of the 'dispositional' barriers that individuals can face when deciding to participate in education: for example, lack of confidence or previous negative experiences of formal education. All in all, many commentators consider technology-based education to be more convenient, motivating and engaging than traditional forms of totally 'face-to-face' provision.

In all these ways, digital education has been heralded as helping more people participate in education and gain the empowering benefits that result from learning. This widening of education participation is seen to be accelerated by a number of recent technological trends. For instance, access to education is associated with the increased ownership of internet-enabled smartphones, especially in regions where levels of computer ownership have traditionally been low. The provision of educational opportunities is seen to have been widened by the ongoing reconstitution of the internet from a broadcast model of passive online content consumption to more active 'read/ write' modes of participation. Alongside these shifts in digital practices and platforms, much of the inherent 'fairness' of digital education is seen to stem from the ever-increasing openness of digital technology development, where content is freely distributed and left open to alteration and reuse in the spirit of 'creative commons' and 'open source'. For many people, then, these models of digital participation constitute a significant shift in how education can be provided – directly challenging proprietary notions such as copyright, pricing, restrictive supply and the monopoly interests of education institutions, publishers and examination boards.

From 'Open Courseware' to 'Holes-in-the-Wall' – examples of democratic digital education

There are numerous examples of this democratizing potential in action. One much-publicized form has been the emergence of 'MOOCs' ('massive open online courses'). MOOCs are university-affiliated courses offered to masses of online learners for little or no cost. Through the rise of providers such as Udacity, edX, Coursera and Futurelearn during the first half of the

2010s, MOOCs were heralded as opening up university-level education to thousands of far-flung students at a time. According to Anant Agarwal – computer science professor at MIT and president of one of the world's largest MOOC providers::

> The MOOC movement is democratizing education. In the past, top universities had this funnel and admitted only the top few per cent of applicants. From the get-go, a lot of students without the right economic or language background were not able to get in. We're flipping the funnel. We're saying everybody can try. If you can cut it, we'll give you a certificate of mastery.[7]

While generating unprecedented levels of publicity in the world of online learning, MOOCs were by no means the first instance of an 'open educational resource'. One notable forerunner was the 'Open Courseware' programme initiated by the Massachusetts Institute of Technology (MIT). At the beginning of the 2000s, MIT made the decision to provide access to its online educational materials free of charge. Thousands of education institutions have since followed this example by making their course content available freely through services such as iTunes U, Academic Earth and Udemy. After the first ten years of its initiative, MIT reckoned that content from over two thousand of its college-level courses had been accessed by around 100 million people. The university has since set a target for a ten-fold increase by 2021, aiming to 'bridge the global gap between human potential and opportunity, so that motivated people everywhere can improve their lives and change the world'.[8]

Alongside these higher education initiatives, efforts to open up compulsory schooling through the internet have also thrived. Online classes and 'cyber schools' are a growing presence in compulsory school systems around the world. The majority of states in the US, for instance, now support individual cyber schools as well as having district-level online programmes where between 20 and 80 per cent of a student's academic instruction can be delivered via the internet. It is reckoned that 315,000 US students are enrolled full-time in state-wide fully online schools, with one million taking online courses each year alongside regular classroom lessons.[9] This online provision is seen to bring high-quality schooling to children and young people who otherwise might be unable to access it. In the words of the largest provider of online schooling in the United States: 'We have the ability to give any student across the state regardless of where they live and regardless of their socioeconomic status the ability to access a public school. That's why online charter schools have been described as the most public of all public schools.'[10]

The idea that digital technology can provide accessible alternatives to conventional schooling has certainly found favour in developing regions. One celebrated example has been the work of Sugata Mitra, who rose to prominence after winning the $1million TED prize in 2013. Mitra started his 'Hole-in-the-Wall' project at the end of the 1990s – cementing internet-enabled computers into the walls of impoverished Indian neighbourhoods. These community computers were left unattended in the hope of giving local children the means through which to self-organize their own technology-based learning. Mitra's initial efforts later developed into the so-called 'School in the Cloud' project, which made use of Skype to connect classrooms in poor communities with volunteer mentors and online resources elsewhere in the world. As the project publicity put it, '[C]hildren, no matter how rich or poor, can engage and connect with information and mentoring online.'[11] While ambitious, Mitra's ideas have proved inspirational throughout the international development sector. In sub-Saharan Africa, for example, the 'Projects for All' charity is now supporting the construction of community-built and community-owned internet access kiosks ('Hello Hubs') to provide computers, servers and Wi-Fi access to local communities.[12] The solar-powered hubs are designed specifically to encourage educational uses of these technologies – particularly by young people and teachers in each community.

Another ambitious example of using digital technology to democratize access to education in developing regions is the 'One Laptop Per Child' (OLPC) initiative. OLPC is a prominent non-profit initiative that has been fronted by MIT professor Nicholas Negroponte since the 2000s. The initiative involved the design and development of low-cost and low-specification laptop and tablet computers – most famously the so-called '$100 Laptop'. These have been distributed throughout some of the poorest regions of the world, and currently over 2.5 million devices have reached children in over thirty countries. OLPC's mission statement is straightforward: 'to empower the world's poorest children through education'.[13] As with Hole-in-the-Wall, Hello Hubs and Open Courseware, providing access to digital resources is intended to be an immediate way of allowing otherwise excluded individuals to learn autonomously from educational content and collaborate with others.

These examples illustrate the tendency of work in the area of education equity and technology to tread a fine line between hope and hubris. This tension is perhaps most evident when digital education initiatives have been launched hurriedly in response to humanitarian disasters. The Haiti earthquake in 2010 spurred donations of OLPC laptops and numerous 'Hack for Haiti' initiatives amongst communities of computer programmers (what some technologists term 'random hacks of kindness'). While less than one per cent of the Haitian population were making regular use of the internet before the earthquake, a number of education technology initiatives were then established on the island – including a 'Digital Literacy for Haiti Rebuilding' programme sponsored by Intel, and the building of forty solar-powered computer labs by the 'Haiti Connected Schools' programme.[14] Another recent example was the series of education technology projects in refugee camps established in the aftermath of conflicts in the Middle East and sub-Saharan Africa. This saw the implementation of ambitious initiatives to bring cheap mini-computer circuit-boards to Syrian refugee camps to teach programming and coding skills.[15] Even more extraordinary was the provision of MOOCs for refugees stranded by the Somalia conflict.[16] As such efforts illustrate, for many technologists and educators, the empowering potential of digital technology knows few limits.

Making a significant difference? Evidence for the democratizing impact of technology

Most of these projects, programmes and initiatives have been enacted with the best of intentions. It therefore feels churlish and mean-spirited to question their effectiveness. That said, proponents of digital education are quick to point to specific successes and 'good news' arising from such work. Many of the examples just described have well-worn success stories that accompany their promotion. Sugata Mitra is fond of recounting the instance of children from a remote fishing village in Southern India who used their local Hole-in-the-Wall to teach themselves sufficient bioscience in seventy-five days to gain scores of 30 per cent on a university end-of-year exam. Similarly, one of the early MOOCs offered by MIT was completed by Battushig Myanganbayar, a fifteen-year-old Mongolian student. Dubbed by the *New*

York Times as the 'boy genius of Ulan Bator', Battushig was said to have earned a perfect score in the MOOC, subsequently enrolling as a full-time undergraduate at MIT's Boston campus. Not only were Battushig's life circumstances transformed, but he was then called upon to advise MIT faculty on how to improve their MOOC provision. As such heart-warming anecdotes imply, one can easily point towards specific cases where digital provision has made a difference to education engagement.

Of course, these anecdotes are no substitute for sustained empirical evidence and analysis. Unfortunately, when digital forms of education provision and engagement are subjected to rigorous scrutiny, their democratizing 'effects' are less easy to identify. For example, while independent studies are scarce, the few research reports that have been conducted on OLPC programmes tend to find little or no effect on children's test scores. A few sustained studies of how the devices were being used *in situ* found children from higher-income families to be making best use of the OLPC devices. These children, it was argued, enjoyed greater support from family members when making sense of the devices and were less concerned than poorer households about damaging or breaking what were relatively expensive objects.[17] Similarly, independent studies in the aftermath of Hole-in-the-Wall programmes have also tended to portray 'low-level learning', internet access that 'rarely functioned' and children disadvantaged by the lack of consideration for content in languages other than English – such as Hindi. As summed up by Mark Warschauer, a seasoned researcher of OLPC and one-to-one laptop programmes, '[M]inimally invasive education was, in practice, minimally effective education.'[18]

These disappointing outcomes extend into other forms of digital education. In the case of MOOCs, for example, analyses of learner data and enrolment analytics tend to suggest that these online courses have enforced rather than overcome educational privilege and exclusivity. Beyond the headline depictions of large classes of diverse, far-flung students, most MOOC participants turn out to be young, well-educated Europeans and North Americans with graduate and postgraduate degrees who often take these courses to gain professional skills.[19] As the Smithsonian concluded, 'Online courses aren't actually democratizing education ... 80 per cent of MOOC students come from the wealthiest and most well educated 6 per cent of the population.'[20] These patterns are exacerbated when one considers the small proportions of enrolled MOOC 'students' who actually remain engaged for the duration of the course. While the average MOOC has been reckoned to enrol around 43,000 participants, best estimates put the proportion of those who actually complete a course at between 4 and 8 per cent. Again, these individuals are more likely to be well educated, Western and from high-income backgrounds.[21]

The tendency for online education to attract the 'usual suspects' – i.e. people already involved extensively in education – is a recurring finding. One retrospective analysis of internet usage by 47,000 UK adults throughout the 2000s showed that while internet access increased by 66 per cent over the decade, people's propensity to engage in education did not. Those individuals who were using the internet to engage with formal or informal learning were most likely to be young, already engaged in some form of educational participation and from relatively advantaged backgrounds.[22] This is not to deny that online courses and educational resources are *increasing* levels of participation in education. However, this is very different to claims of *widening* participation to individuals and groups who were previously marginalized and excluded.

There is also growing evidence that people's experiences of digital education are patterned distinctly in terms of social class, race and disability. For example, studies are beginning to illustrate the ways in which online learning environments do not unproblematically reduce differences between individuals. The US sociologist Tressie McMillan Cottom has conducted research into the online learning experiences of black and ethnic minority students. This suggests that few opportunities exist for such 'participants' to bring their cultural backgrounds into online learning experiences as they encounter and make sense of content. Cottom argues that online systems get designed and configured to 'the norm' of a self-motivated, highly able individual who is 'disembodied from place, culture, history, markets, and inequality regimes'.[23] When online learning systems (and, to an extent, other online students) encounter students who do not conform to this norm, they tend to find fault. Put bluntly, when learning online, it still matters very much who one is. The social disadvantages of being black, female, poor and/or having a physical or intellectual disability do not simply disappear when one learns through the internet.

Overall, then, there is little sustained evidence of any wholesale democratization of education through digital technologies. While some disadvantaged individuals undoubtedly gain much through their engagement with digital education, this is not usually replicated on a wide scale across populations. Digital technologies might not be making things worse, but neither are they making things much better. If anything, the limited patterns of participation and benefit associated with online learning, MOOCs, and so on, could be said to replicate what is known as the 'Matthew Effect' (referring to the gospel of Matthew's declaration that 'whosoever hath, to him shall be given, and he shall have more abundance: but whosoever hath not, from him shall be taken away').[24] The phenomenon of initial advantages multiplying over time can be found across many areas of society such as science, technology and politics.[25] We perhaps should not be surprised that digital education appears broadly to follow suit. As Kentaro Toyama concludes:

If educational inequality is the main issue, then no amount of digital technology will turn things around. . . . Technology amplifies preexisting differences in wealth and achievement. Children with greater vocabularies get more out of Wikipedia. Students with behavioral challenges are more distracted by video games. Rich parents will pay for tutors so that their children can learn to program the devices that others merely learn to use. Technology at school may level the playing field of access, but a level field does nothing to improve the skill of the players, which is the whole point of education.[26]

Reasons for these 'failures' of digital democracy

In sum, digital education does not appear to lead to wholly 'fair' forms of democracy. Increasing opportunities for the well-resourced, highly motivated, already-educated classes certainly falls short of more radical ideals of 'improving the odds', being a 'great equalizer' or 'flipping the funnel'. These shortfalls between the democratic promises of digital education and the actual outcomes should not be ignored. Instead, we need to take time to unpack the possible reasons why the democratic potential of digital technology is realized rarely – if at all – on a sustained basis. While there is no straightforward answer, these relative failures of digital democracy relate (at least in part) to different understandings and expectations of what can be achieved through digital technology.

When making sense of the democratizing potential of digital education, there is a need to be clear about what sorts of 'fairness' and 'democracy' are being talked about. In particular, we need to remain mindful of the fundamental differences between *equality* and *equity*. On one hand, equality relates to the desire to make sure that everyone gets the same things that might be required to live one's life to the full. In terms of digital education, therefore, equality tends to involve making sure that all people have the same opportunities to access and participate in education through digital technologies. This thinking underpins many of the attempts outlined in this chapter to make education 'fairer' – such as giving devices to all young people or providing online courses free of charge. Initiatives such as these are generally seen to give everybody a fair crack of the (digital) whip.

This approach can work well if everyone is starting from the same place and has similar needs and requirements to succeed. Yet such a uniformity of circumstance is rarely – if ever – the case in real life. If large segments of society already suffer from various forms of disadvantage and exclusion, then it makes little sense to expect 'fairness' and 'democracy' to result simply from providing equal access to digital education. Many of the residual 'unfairnesses' of education outlined at the start of this chapter correspond to the general inequalities of society. In short, it is naïve to assume that everyone has equal choices and equal options. Any serious concern with reducing inequalities is perhaps better directed towards developing *equitable* forms of digital education.

Equitable approaches to digital education are concerned with ensuring that everyone gets whatever different things they might personally require to live life to the full. Crucially, these are needs and requirements that differ depending on a person's circumstances. This relates to the idea of 'social justice', popularized by the philosopher John Rawls. Instead of striving to provide everybody with the same opportunities, social justice stresses the need for individuals to be each given an *effective* equal chance of realizing their potential when compared to anyone else in similar circumstances and with similar abilities. The key concern here is making sure that people who are already disadvantaged are given appropriate assistance in overcoming those disadvantages: that is, what is labelled 'redistribution of opportunities', 'affirmative action' or 'positive discrimination'. Equitable forms of digital education might include giving the most disadvantaged students their own technological devices, but will also involve training to use them, ongoing technical support to troubleshoot any problems that arise, and perhaps financial assistance with the cost of their upkeep.

Clearly, many of the 'democratizing' forms of digital education initiatives outlined in this chapter are focused on matters of equality rather than equity. As such, they can hardly be expected to overcome pre-existing inequalities and divisions, or buck the trend of the Matthew Effect. Many people in positions of power and responsibility are relatively happy to support the idea of equal access and giving all individuals the same chances to succeed through their own ability and hard work. After all, the notion that 'all men are created equal' lies at the heart of historical Western understandings of democracy and individual freedom. In contrast, the idea of advantaging some people over others is a less comfortable approach for many to pursue – even when it means giving more help to those who need it most. Libertarians and/or advocates of the free market would see little or no sense in intervening in this manner.

As such, any 'democratizing' potential of digital education is often compromised by tensions that persist in many societies between ideals of individual freedom and ideals of social equality. In addition is the fact that effective educational participation depends on much more than ease of access alone. Key here is the complex nature of what could be termed 'equality of condition'. In short, there are many things that need to be addressed in order for education to be made 'fairer' and for people to have 'real options' and be equally enabled and empowered.[27] These include inequalities of income and resources, social networks and relationships, pressures of time, health, family demands and working conditions. These also include less tangible differences in the extent to which individuals benefit from equal rights and are fulfilled in terms of basic human needs for care, love and solidarity. Clearly, there is much here that will not be addressed purely through online courses and $100 laptops.

Conclusions

Given these caveats, it is hardly surprising that efforts to render education more 'democratic' or 'fair' through digital means are falling short. Of course, judging whether technology is a democratizing force in education depends upon one's values and ideology. Digital education is clearly 'a good thing' if one believes in increasing basic opportunities and access but is less concerned about the 'winners' and 'losers' who 'naturally' result – what is often referred to as a belief in meritocracy. On the other hand, if one considers the levels of inequality that persist in the digital age to be unacceptable, then there is clearly more work to be done. This is what was referred to earlier as 'social justice'. As Kalwant Bhopal and Farzana Shain put it: '[S]ocial justice in education is not just about equality in the distribution of, or access to, an educational service, which is important, but "social justice concerns the nature of the service itself and its consequences for society through time".'[28] In other words, the democratizing of education along socially just lines requires more than access and opportunity. Instead, attention needs to be paid to the things that happen to people during their engagements with digital education and as a result of their engagements with digital education. In these terms, digital education reinforces and reproduces particular forms of democracy and privilege, as well as particular forms of inequality and disadvantage. If one looks beyond the instrumentalist act of increasing the diversity of education opportunities, then there is little reason to celebrate technology's democratizing effect.

Equity and social justice are complex issues that require looking far beyond the digital. As such, the most realistic approaches to making education 'fair' are those that are also focused on making society 'fair'. Addressing fundamental issues of poverty, prejudice and discrimination is a prerequisite to any digital democratization of education. As the educational philosopher Douglas Kellner reflected:

> [T]echnology itself does not necessarily improve teaching and learning, and will certainly not of itself overcome acute socioeconomic divisions. Indeed, without proper re-visioning of education and without adequate resources, pedagogy, and educational practices, technology could be an obstacle or burden to genuine learning and will probably increase rather than overcome existing divisions of power, cultural capital, and wealth.[29]

This is not to argue that we should give up completely on the democratic potential of digital technology. Technology clearly offers alternatives to the limited choices that many people find themselves faced with. Yet this *is* to argue that the promises being made on behalf of digital education need to be more realistic when it comes to the complex nature of inequality and disadvantage. Digital technology might be part of a solution to overcome social disadvantage, but it should never be seen as *the* solution. This seems like an obvious enough proposition when written down in black and white, but is easy to lose sight of amidst the hype and hopes that surround the digital education bandwagon.

THREE

Making Education More Personalized?

Introduction

Digital technology is often sold on the grounds of supporting individuals to do what they want (and need) to do. This sentiment certainly lies behind some memorable sales pitches from the IT industry: 'Where Do You Want To Go Today?' (Microsoft); 'The Possibilities Are Infinite' (Fujitsu); 'Think Different' and 'The Power To Be Your Best' (Apple). Often the idea of fitting digital technology around personal needs and desires is built into the nature and form of the actual devices. The user of any computer or smartphone, for example, is expected to personalize many of their machine's defining features. Screensavers, display backgrounds, colour schemes, icons and fonts can all be customized endlessly. Users are also encouraged to reconfigure ringtones, error messages and the manner in which devices are illuminated, vibrate, start up and shut down. Digital hardware can also be augmented through the installation of apps, software programs, additional chips, memory cards, different casings, plug-ins and other 'add-ons'. Once taken out of their packaging, smartphones, tablets and computers are designed to feel like intimate personal possessions rather than mass-produced consumer goods.

The bespoke nature of digital devices is symptomatic of a general turn throughout contemporary society and culture. In the wake of the growing business practice throughout the 1980s of selling customized and tailored services, personalization spread during the 1990s and 2000s into government and public services, and now is a regular feature of everyday life. These forms of personalization take a variety of forms. On one hand is the provision of 'customer-friendly' interfaces and similar methods of increasing people's choices in how they navigate through services. On the other hand is the practice of allowing individuals to 'co-design' and 'co-produce' services, or even self-organize completely.[1] All these types of 'personalization' reflect a common philosophy of allowing different people to do different things in order to reach the same goal or outcome.

Digital technologies underpin many of the ways in which personalized practices have become woven into the fabric of modern life. For example, cheap digital printing and large-scale display technologies mean that we are now accustomed to niche marketing campaigns targeting specific groups and communities. Advertisers have also begun to explore methods of 'predictive personalization' that analyse what is known about recent purchases, online activities and interactions to predict customers' future needs and desires. Online retailers such as Amazon.com are adept at making personal 'suggestions' on the basis of previous searching and purchasing behaviours. Now companies are developing algorithmic means of calculating when customers do things that suggest imminent changes, such as pregnancy, divorce or moving house.

Personalization is a key feature of the consumption as well as selling of goods and services. Growing numbers of products are purchased on the basis of 'mass customization': that is, where the appearance and functionality of standardized items can be configured by the consumer. For example, shoppers on the Nike website can (re-)design the size, colour, material, logos and slogans of their new shoes. Similar shifts have occurred in the differentiated and personalized ways that news, information and entertainment are consumed digitally. Substantial proportions of the television audience now view programmes 'on demand' rather than on a pre-scheduled 'linear' basis. Many people's online consumption of news and information is filtered by personal preferences – reflecting Nicholas Negroponte's prediction over twenty years ago that internet users would move away from mass media in favour of online news feeds customized to each individual's tastes and interests (what he termed 'The Daily Me').[2]

Significantly, these differentiated modes of production and consumption have also become established in what were previously considered to be monolithic public services and professions. For example, healthcare systems are adjusting to the emergence of 'personalized medicine' where medical decisions, treatments and interventions are tailored through computerized analyses of individual patients' molecular and genetic make-up. There has also been a growth of personalized government services over the past decade or so, particularly through the development of decentralized and 'molecular' online services.[3] Such changes in the public and private sectors are heralded as combining the efficiency of mass production with the aim of meeting individual needs and choice. From heart surgery to sneakers, the idea that 'one size fits all' is being turned on its head, with digital technologies at the centre of much of this change.

The digital personalization of education

It is understandable that technology-driven personalization has begun to appear in education. Of course,
digital personalization is preceded by a rich tradition
in twentieth-century education of making teaching
and learning more 'learner centred'. This is evident, for
example, in the enduring philosophies of 'progressive
teaching', 'Montessori education' and the 'free school'
movement that continues through institutions such
as Summerhill. Parallels can also be drawn with the
continued popularity of 'home schooling', especially
amongst groups who feel under-served by mass education systems. Similarly, the policy concept of 'lifelong
learning' rose to prominence during the 1990s in
recognition of education being directed by individuals
over the course of their lifetimes rather than being the
preserve of any particular institution.

Set against these developments, the expectation
that technology can support individually driven and
'learner-centred' forms of education makes good
sense. Indeed, long-standing principles of self-man-
agement and learner autonomy live on in a number of
different ways through digital education. First is the
idea that technologies might personalize key elements
of 'formal' education such as schools, universities,

examination systems, and so on. In theory these 'official' forms of personalization involve a complete reordering of education systems and institutions:

> The logic of education systems should be reversed so that it is the system that conforms to the learner, rather than the learner to the system. This is the essence of personalization. It demands a system capable of offering bespoke support for each individual that recognizes and builds upon their diverse strengths, interests, abilities and needs in order to foster engaged and independent learners able to reach their full potential.[4]

In practice, digital technologies have been used to rearrange and reform a number of different elements of 'mass' education provision. For example, 'digital portfolios' and 'e-portfolios' are now used widely in schools and colleges to support students in amassing and arranging online collections of their own work for eventual assessment. This individualized curation is intended to encourage students to include evidence of learning that might not have been part of any formal curriculum, while also reflecting on what they have done and what might require further development. Many schools and colleges are also exploring the digital personalization of curricula. This includes the use of digital technology to support 'personalized learning strategies' where students can concentrate on subjects and topics that they are particularly interested in. Short online quizzes and tests are used to monitor and diagnose progress, as well as pointing students towards appropriate subsequent activities.

Such technology use is growing across all levels of education. Respected universities such as University of California, Davis have introduced adaptive introductory courses where online content is presented to students according to their own learning strengths and weaknesses. These principles also underpin the growing use of adaptive online testing throughout elementary and high school systems. Here, online systems alter the content and difficulty of questions in light of each student's initial performance. Such tests are beginning to be used for 'high-stakes' examinations, such as Australia's nationwide NAPLAN (National Assessment Program – Literacy and Numeracy) tests. This approach allows examinations to be focused on measuring what an individual student actually knows and understands rather than what they do not.

Such approaches have led to the establishment of entire institutions around personalized principles.

One early example of this is AltSchool, founded by an ex-head of Google's 'personalization team' and backed by hundreds of millions of dollars of investment from investor groups and philanthropists such as Mark Zuckerberg. AltSchool is conceived as a chain of small private schools based around principles of personalized engagement. This entails students all engaging with different knowledge and content at individualized rates of progression. Each school is staffed by its own software engineers responsible for crafting bespoke technology responses to issues and challenges as they arise. The philosophy of AltSchool is to 'go far beyond the conventional "one size fits all" approach to education'.[5] As the AltSchool founder put it:

> I was running the Google personalization team prior to joining AltSchool, and most of the original group of people starting AltSchool, on the technical side, are from that team. We believe that personalization and customization is the way to go in any environment, whether you're talking about medicine or automotive – even food. It is the best of scale and the best of individualization. We believe that humans are very similarly made, but also absolutely unique in other ways; personalization is

the way to strike that balance. Within the school context, personalization is incredibly important because it actually meets each child where they are and motivates them and makes the best use of the precious time that they have in school. The environment that they're going to live in for their entire adult lives is one where they're not told what to do. They have to understand themselves and what they need to be happy and successful. We let them chart their own path in a way that leaves the people around them better off. That's a personalized experience.[6]

While innovative, such examples still retain the idea of education taking place within schools, colleges and universities – albeit with digital technology acting to differentiate the experience. More radical, perhaps, is the use of digital technology to support efforts to establish education as something that takes place completely outside of any specific institution. These 'unofficial' forms of personalized digital education acknowledge the many different ways that an individual might learn through digital technology. For example, the term 'personalized learning environment' is used increasingly to reflect the ways that many people now access information and interact with others through collections of disparate online applications and channels. This includes the 'personalized learning technologies' that different individuals might be using, such as Twitter, blogging, and so on. It also encompasses the 'personalized learning networks' that are sustained by these technologies: that is, the people and resources that any individual can connect with through these technologies.

Attempts are being made to develop forms of education that rely upon individuals' use of personal technologies and networks. Rather than focusing on specific classes or topics, students are given responsibility to organize, direct and control their own learning activities as they see fit. Rather than all students producing the same piece of final assessment work, some online courses simply assess an aggregation of the relevant online activities that each student has engaged in. Evidence of each student's 'success' might be based on the sum of their tweets, blog posts, forum discussions and/or video uploads. This certainly contrasts with the 'paternalistic' expectation of many formal courses that all students will use the same tools and have the same interactions. As Annika Rensfeldt reasons, basing education around personal technological tools and networks could be seen as marking 'a radical shift in favour of the individual learner, where personalisation is considered to challenge the dominant view of the enclosed, mass treatment by educational institutions'.[7]

Such approaches certainly reflect the variety of freely distributed and professionally produced learning resources that can be found online. For instance, video lectures and other instructional content are available freely through well-respected channels such as iTunes U and Khan Academy, alongside thousands of lesser-known equivalents. Now, it is argued, anyone can provide online courses without the institutional support of a recognized college or university. Platforms such as Udemy host thousands of such 'renegade professors'. As Jeffrey Young observes, 'This is what happens when the so-called sharing economy meets education – when the do-it-yourself spirit of Silicon Valley is applied to teaching.'[8] Many of these platforms are recognized as offering high-quality learning opportunities equivalent to the elite providers of previous eras. For example, TED talks have been described in glowing terms as 'a new Harvard – the first new top-prestige education brand in more than 100 years'.[9]

Beyond these fêted providers lie a range of other learning opportunities. These include the MOOCs discussed in chapter 2, as well as the radically spirited online efforts of 'Free Universities' such as the Melbourne Free University and Université Populaire de Caen. All told, digital technology enables a vast 'learning black market' far beyond the reaches of the traditional education system.[10] It is perfectly possible for someone to now look past the offer of studying for a conventional degree or diploma, and instead curate their own education as they see fit. As Dale Stephens – leading light of the 'Uncollege' movement – asserts boldly: 'Universities do not exist to train you for the real world; they exist to make money. If you want to learn the skills required to navigate the world – the hustle, networking and creativity – you're going to have to hack your own education.'[11]

Perceived benefits of the digital personalization of education

Personalized digital education has been welcomed as an obvious way around many of the problems inherent in 'cookie cutter' models of mass education provision. The technologies just described are spearheading a resurgence of personalized reform in current education policy-making and governance. Many schools and university systems are being remodelled steadily around increased choice and diversity of provision. Accreditation of prior learning, adaptive curricula and assessment are becoming increasingly accepted in even the most traditional corners of formal education. Powerful voices now advocate reframing core aspects of education around the needs, preferences and opinion of individual students. As the Bill & Melinda Gates Foundation has put it, 'Learning becomes even more powerful when it is personalized to each student's needs, interests, and circumstances.'[12]

All of the digital technologies outlined so far in this chapter have therefore been welcomed as contributing to a much-needed 'reboot' of education, moving the provision of teaching and learning closer to the expectations of contemporary society. Often this realignment is framed in consumerist terms, with digital technologies seen to bring the personalized ethos of popular online services to bear on education sectors that have historically been unconcerned with their 'customers'. As Newt Gingrich has argued:

> Teachers lecture, students sit and some listen. Class happens at the same time, with the same material, and at the same pace for everyone. This is an 1890s model of education – teaching to the 'average' student, rather than the individual. In an age when

most information and knowledge is transmitted digitally and is increasingly personalized – think about how Netflix, Pandora, Twitter and Facebook work – we should be able to do much better than that. Pioneering projects like Khan Academy, Udacity and Coursera are pointing toward a future of learning that is more like Netflix than the chalk-and-textbook system we have today. Each of them is using technology to help students learn at their own pace, on their own path, and toward their own goals.[13]

Gingrich's popularist sentiments are broadly in line with expert opinion on the psychology of learning and education. For example, the idea of a technology-based 'pick-and-mix' approach to educational engagement chimes with theoretical accounts in the learning sciences and cognitive psychology of learner-centred and student-centred education. Humanist psychology has long subscribed to the belief that individuals operate best when given responsibility for developing their own perceptions, values, feelings and behaviours. In this sense, the individual is considered best placed to direct and take charge of their own learning. As Carl Rogers reasoned in his theory of 'self-actualization': 'As no one else can know how we perceive, we are the best experts on ourselves.'[14] From this basis, ideas of self-directed and independent learning have become widely accepted in mainstream education thinking over the past fifty years.

Technology-driven personalization also has clear parallels with other popular educational theories of the past few decades. For example, theories of 'self-regulated learning' stress the importance of individuals being able continually to monitor their own progress, identify strengths and weaknesses and plan strategic ways forward to adapt and improve. This reflexive state of educational involvement is seen to require that an individual receives frequent feedback about their learning. In this sense, digital technology has been celebrated by Barry Zimmerman – one of the movement's founding theorists – as 'render[ing] new forms of self-regulated learning practical'.[15]

As well as complementing received wisdoms about learning, personalized education technologies also fit neatly with the ways in which digital technology supports people to interact and work with others, and the changing nature of what constitutes 'community' in an era of 'always on' connectivity. The idea of personalized and individualized technology-based education certainly corresponds to the ways that networked technologies allow individuals to transcend limitations of proximity and circumstance, and connect to what-ever and whomever they wish. This is not to say that individuals are completely alone and isolated in their online activities – after all, one of the strengths of digital technology is its ability to bring crowds, 'swarms' and 'mobs' of like-minded people together. Rather, digital media are celebrated as supporting new forms of individualized communities that are less per-manent, more fluid and loosely based around fleeting associations and commonalities of interests.

Many of the 'unofficial' forms of personalized digital education described earlier therefore embody what Lee Rainie and Barry Wellman have termed 'networked individualism'. This is the understand-ing that through social and networked technologies, individuals benefit from being able to dip in and out of loosely knit social circles of other networked individuals. Digital technologies constitute what Rainie and Wellman term an alternative 'operating system' through which people connect, communi-cate, work together, create and share content and exchange information. These are all highly personal arrangements with the individual 'at the autonomous center'. This state of networked individualism is seen to 'expand opportunities for learning, problem solving, decision making, and personal interaction'.[16]

The idea of personalized digital education is certainly supported by the ways in which many commentators see technology-saturated society taking shape. Alongside the idea of 'networked individualization', the concept of personalized digital education echoes various (often contradictory) contemporary political viewpoints and ideological stances centred on the primacy of the individual. On one hand are progressive ideals that education should be democratic and respectful of individual differences and needs. In this sense, educational participation needs to be (re)arranged around principles of personal liberties, self-responsibility and self-improvement.[17] On the other hand, the notion of technology-based personalized education also fits well with 'neo-liberal' concerns over the need to reorganize public services around individual choice and flexibility of provision. Thus, rather than following a predetermined pathway, every individual should be free to consume education in an 'entrepreneurial' manner – calculating risks, working out what is most appropriate and then acting accordingly. From this perspective, education is best arranged around the economic ideas of 'rational choice' and market forces.

Similarly, technology-based personalized education chimes with 'libertarian' sensibilities that have grown in cultural prominence over the past twenty years – especially in North America. In particular are beliefs that society should be based primarily around 'the personal', with each individual citizen free to exercise their personal rights and choices to meet their personal needs or characteristics. Principles of self-determination and self-sufficiency are valued above reliance on large institutions, government and the state. Such ideas have fuelled the rising popularity of movements as diverse as the Tea Party, 'rugged individualism' and 'maker culture'. These ideologies share considerable common ground with the basic logic of technology-based personalized education. The idea of making education more personalized through technology therefore corresponds to a number of popular philosophies and political movements that would otherwise appear to be at odds with each other. This is clearly a form of education that addresses a diverse range of concerns and demands.

Thinking against the digital personalization of education

Set against this background, it is wholly understandable that personalized forms of digital education are believed by many educators and experts to be an essentially 'good thing'. Indeed, it is rare to find arguments against the individual 'freedoms' of learning through technology. This is, however, not to presume that serious caveats do not exist. First, from a technical point of view, many of the most popular and most profitable forms of 'personalized' learning could be criticized as being little more than 'mass customization' through large systems. Just as Nike allows its online customers to make adjustments to the surface appearance of what remain essentially the same sneakers, many personalized 'bespoke' learning systems are concerned primarily with delivering predetermined content to students, albeit in different sequences and various forms of presentation. Any ideals of infinite 'differences' and 'freedoms' are constrained in practice by predesigned systems and finite content. The eventual outcomes of the applications and systems outlined in this chapter could be seen as just as 'one size fits all' as the systems they purport to displace. How 'personalized' and individually centred are systems where everyone still ends up learning the same Physics 101 syllabus (even if they believe that they are personally choosing to do so)? As Jodi Dean reflects, 'Personalization should thus not be confused with personal. There is nothing personal here.'[18]

Second, the diversity of online education provision that does exist outside of formal education (what was described earlier as the 'learning black market') is tempered by a corresponding lack of guidance and support. The assumption that all individuals can navigate their own pathways through digital education opportunities implies a corresponding withdrawal of expert direction, guidance and support. While offering an alternative to the perceived paternalism of organized education provision, this approach does bump up against the widely held belief in education that learning is a social endeavour that is best supported by more knowledgeable others. In particular, it could be argued that there are many things that individuals are highly unlikely to discover or explore for themselves – not least because learners 'can't know what they don't know'.[19]

For example, an appreciation of the value of a knowledge domain such as science or maths (and, more importantly, the motivation for engaging in science or maths learning) is not something that can be discovered and recognized spontaneously by all individuals. Rather, it could be argued that the support of mediating experts (such as teachers, mentors, coaches and other 'educators') remains a crucial element in stimulating people to engage with these areas of education and then determine what is worth learning. In this sense, education could be seen as something that demands a 'time for telling' as well as a 'time for discovering' knowledge.[20] Despite having fallen out of fashion in most discussions of digital education, formal teacher-led instruction might often be the most appropriate means by which learning takes place.

Third, the notion of individuals taking responsibility for the success (and failure) of their education also raises a number of social concerns. In particular, the idea of people 'entrepreneurially' picking and choosing their way through a diverse range of education 'opportunities' has divisive connotations. Put bluntly, the principles of the free market suggest that some individuals will be more successful in their decision-making than others. Moreover, every success or failure will be framed primarily as resulting from that individual's actions. This is a model of education participation where a person is ultimately 'on their own' for better and for worse. As Vicky Duckworth and Matthew Cochrane contend, this way of organizing educational participation

position[s] individuals as entrepreneurs managing their own life and responsible for their success or lack of it. In this climate learners are expected to succeed against the odds and if they do not, the fault is their own and not structural inequalities many encounter at each step of their learning journey and indeed life.[21]

As this mention of 'structural inequalities' implies, the expectation of everyone being able to exercise a genuinely free choice in their engagement with education is naïve, if not disingenuous. One does not have to be a sociologist to recognize that we live in 'structured' social environments where choices are bounded, contained and tempered by who we are. As Zygmunt Bauman puts it, everyone in society has choices, but these are inevitably bounded by 'fate' – that is, circumstances 'over which we have no influence: things "happening to us" that are not of our doing (such as the geographical place and the social location into which we were born, or the time of our birth)'.[22] Of course, any individual can strive to influence the ways in which their 'fate' plays out through hard work, training and cultivating their talents – actions that Bauman describes as 'character'. Yet what an individual can realistically 'choose' to do remains dictated by a combination of character and circumstances. All the forms of educational choice outlined in this chapter are clearly going to benefit some people more than others.

This brings us back to the observations made in

chapter 2 regarding the likelihood of digital education advantaging those who are already advantaged. Tressie McMillan Cottom reiterates this concern succinctly with regard to the harsh realities of digital education for 'minority' groups. In particular, she describes how personalized forms of online education have become configured steadily around the ideal of what she terms the 'roaming autodidact'.[23] These are individuals who have the requisite confidence, motivation, technologies and educational credentials to breeze their way through Khan Academy, MOOCs, TED talks and similar digital education opportunities. These are individuals who are economically comfortable, well resourced and time-rich. These are individuals who are well positioned in the 'market' to be nimble, to be nomadic and to act generally in the 'flexible' manner that we are told is advantageous in the digital age. These are clearly *not* circumstances that are enjoyed by every individual.

Conclusions

Much of what has been discussed in this chapter reflects a common concern over the public qualities of digital education. If we are all immersed in our own

'If we are all immersed in our own personalized learning journeys, what implications might this have for education as a social, supportive and shared endeavour?'

personalized learning journeys, what implications might this have for education as a social, supportive and shared endeavour? This is not to dismiss technology-based personalization and individualization as a completely 'bad thing'. Digital technology undoubtedly is a powerful means of supporting different people to do different things in different ways. Yet the question that arises throughout this chapter is straightforward enough: to what extent is education compromised when reframed as a digitally based 'free-for-all'?

Of course, the orthodoxy of personalization that currently pervades many areas of society makes arguing against personalized digital education a difficult task. After all, Western societies are predicated upon ideas of freedom and being able to do things 'our own way'. Much of the ever-increasing centrality of digital technology to modern life is based around promises of individual wish fulfilment. As such, it can feel uncomfortable to argue against the seductive appeal of 'living in a world made only of one's wishes; of mine and yours, of our – the buyers, consumers, users and beneficiaries of technology – wants and wishes'.[24]

The idea of doing what we want and doing it on our own terms has obvious allure. This is especially the case with regard to education – particularly for those who might have had frustrating experiences of 'mass' and/or 'compulsory' education in the form of schools, colleges and universities. In this sense, the ideals of personalized digital education speak directly to many people's inner adolescent. These are propositions that also appeal to a narcissistic belief that our own experiences are somehow more important than the experiences of most others. It could therefore be argued that much of the passionate support that many people show for personalized digital education is very personalized in its origins. Wanting to satisfy these base individualistic impulses through the latest technology is understandable. Yet is this really the most equitable basis for the wholesale reform of education?

It is also important to force ourselves to question the role that personalized digital education plays in reframing education around market values, the language of consumer choice and the idea of learning as 'product'. Many of the examples outlined in this chapter constitute forms of 'education' that are packaged neatly for the 'consumer society' with its emphasis on self-expression and lifestyle choices through individualistic acts of consumption. As just argued, these are difficult values in contemporary society to refute. Yet, given the public significance of education, these are values that certainly deserve more scrutiny. In particular, this reintroduces one of the questions raised towards the end of chapter 1: that is, what are the potential losses here? The prospect of refashioning teaching and learning in the image of Netflix might make sound sense in the mind of Newt Gingrich, but surely overlooks some of the fundamental qualities, characteristics and values of what makes for 'good' education.

FOUR

Making Education More Calculable?

Introduction

Another technological development that many people
see as a potential 'good' for education is digital data.
Of course, 'data' are not a new societal phenomenon
– measurements, observations and statistics have been
collected and analysed for administrative purposes since
the 1700s. Yet the generation and processing of data
through digital technologies (notably computers) is
now taking place on an unprecedented scale. This
step change has been described in terms of the 'three
Vs' of volume, variety and velocity: that is, increases
in the amounts of data that are now being generated;
the range of data types and sources in existence; and
the speed with which these data are produced and
processed.[1] Given the 'deluge' of digital data witnessed
across various areas of society over the past ten years
or so, many commentators are anticipating a future
defined increasingly through data, algorithms, coding
and analytics.

Digital forms of data are embedded throughout everyday life. For example, data are integral to the technological devices that we carry around constantly and use at home, work and all points in between. Great swathes of data are generated, stored and shared through our use of social media and cloud computing. Conversely, vast amounts of data are generated by the many surveillance applications and tracking devices that are embedded in day-to-day settings and practices. Data are also central to the computerized administrative systems that drive the operations of large organizations, public institutions and state bureaucracies. This abundance of data will increase with the development of the so-called 'internet of things' and the integration of internet-connected sensors and data-generation devices into everyday objects. In addition, computational tools and techniques are being developed to facilitate the processing of 'big data', where vast data sets are joined together and analysed through large-scale and highly complex calculations.

Although less contentious (and newsworthy) than the rise of data in science, business and government, digital data are certainly a significant feature of contemporary education. Even the most traditional of schools, colleges and universities now functions along continuous 'data-driven' lines, with masses of data being generated, processed and analysed through digital technologies on a daily basis. These data range from *ad hoc* 'in-house' monitoring of students and teachers to the systematic 'public' collection of data at local, state and federal levels. In addition, huge amounts of 'naturally occurring' data are generated and scrutinized from the daily use of 'virtual learning environments' and other forms of online learning that log information from every key-stroke, mouse-click and screen-swipe. In various forms, then, digital data are seen to underpin new forms of educational provision and organization that are more measurable, calculable and perhaps even controllable.

Examples of the data turn in education

In order to appreciate the full extent of this 'datafication' of contemporary education, it is helpful to consider some specific examples. Data, coding and algorithms lie at the heart of a range of recent education developments. For instance, commercially produced 'talent management' software is now used in schools to aid teacher recruitment and retention through data-driven 'teacher evaluation and performance' monitoring. Some schools are investing in 'data analytic platforms' that facilitate the regular grading of teachers and lessons by students, thereby producing steady streams of metrics, measures and feedback for the refinement of subsequent provision. As the *New York Times* observed, the increasing popularity of such services 'suggests that techniques pioneered by the tech industry – including the collection and analysis of large troves of data – may help address problems in American education'.[2] Dwarfing the scale of these previous examples is the growing trend for national governments to use institution-level data to drive school comparison websites, where 'key performance indicators' and other data are posted publicly with the intention that families, employers and other 'consumers' of education will make more 'informed' choices and decisions.

Beyond increasing the visibility of educational data, a number of systems have been developed to automate key educational processes through the manipulation of data. One long-standing example of this is the development of automated grading systems. This is software designed to grade essays and assignments automatically, essentially dealing with the statistical modelling and classification of large bodies of text into single numbers and grades. While there has been a long tradition in education of true/false and multiple-choice tests being graded by machine, the assessment of written text had always been considered too big a challenge. Yet recent advances in data-processing and analytic techniques are now supporting the emergence of automated essay-scoring systems into mainstream education. Demand for this technology stems from the increased prominence of high-stakes testing in school systems, tutorless forms of self-directed learning and large-scale online courses with thousands of students all producing assignments that require grading (such as the MOOCs discussed in chapter 2).

Computerized grading systems are a good example of data processing and algorithmic automation – drawing on techniques from the fields of natural language processing, computational linguistics and machine learning. These systems usually start with a sample of human-graded assignments, which are then used to develop complex mathematical models by analysing each essay in terms of word use, semantics, text structure and organization. A process of 'machine reading' then takes place, where artificial intelligence techniques are used to calibrate subsequent grading decisions as and when additional assignments are entered in the system and analysed in terms of their semantic structure and form. While such systems can be criticized for their lack of nuanced 'expert' judgement, this automated data-based process is reckoned to be as valid, reliable and fair as a human grader (if not more so). Computer graders are seen to be more consistent than their human counterparts, less prone to fatigue and able to provide instant feedback in comparison to the weeks (or months) required by many professors and tutors.

The use of data-based techniques to support educational decisions and judgements that were made previously by humans has also expanded in the guise of 'learning analytics'. This is described broadly as 'the measurement, collection, analysis and reporting of data about learners and their contexts, for purposes of understanding and optimizing learning and the environments in which it occurs'.[3] Learning analytics aims to make use of the data trails produced by users of virtual learning environments, learning management systems and other forms of online education. These data can be aggregated and analysed to characterize and categorize information about students' past actions and model predictions of their likely future success (or otherwise). Learning analytic tools often compare a student's actions with other members of their class or group, students from previous cohorts or even abstracted models of 'ideal' performance.

These insights are then presented back to individual students to help them gauge their own progress. These data can also help educators intervene in the case of individuals who are at risk of not progressing to the best of their ability.

Learning analytics represents the educational application of tools and techniques from the fields of 'business intelligence', website analytics and information visualization. Analytics software is encountered most commonly in the form of personalized 'dashboards' which present students with graphs, tables and other visualizations of their learning. These 'sense-making' tools are seen to provide individuals with fine-grained feedback. Some people see these data as providing 'soft interventions' and 'nudges', or even making the process of learning into a game-like activity.[4] Analytics software is also used to model a learner's understanding of a specific topic and adapt the presentation of subsequent content accordingly – what is sometimes referred to as an 'intelligent curriculum'. In all these ways, learning analytics is argued to be able to track larger amounts of data than human educators, to provide faster feedback and, crucially, to identify unexpected patterns and factors.

While many applications of learning analytics are localized in their focus, interest is also rising in the

analysis of large volumes of 'big data' that are generated through mass forms of online learning.[5] Many
large-scale online education systems are designed to
maximize the analytic potential of their usage data. As
Sal Khan – founder of Khan Academy – put it when
justifying his company's strategy of offering its online
learning resources free of charge, 'Data is the real
asset.'[6] One high-profile example of big-data-driven
education is the Knewton 'adaptive learning system'.
This is a 'recommender system' which uses large-scale
data techniques to calculate what form of learning
each of its 15 million enrolled students should be
taking part in, the education resource or service they
should be using, and when and how they should be
learning. Knewton links students to a wide range
of partner education providers, from the University
of Arizona to corporations such as Pearson. Once a
student logs on to a course or tutorial through the
Knewton system, the company's data engine collects
data on every click, scroll, key-stroke, pause and other
interaction. These data are used to model various
aspects of the student's learning, such as their motivation, proficiency and more contested measures such
as 'learning style'. These profiles of students' learning
are then used to recommend the most appropriate
and productive educational step that each student

should take next. The strength of this approach is seen to lie in the vast quantity of data being analysed. As Knewton claims: 'It's fair to say that we have more than a million data points for each student who's taking a Knewton platform course for a semester. That's just the raw click stream data. After the raw data goes through our models, there's exponentially more data that we've produced.'[7]

These innovations are not confined to online education. The large amounts of data, data-enabling digital devices and data-driven practices within 'bricks and mortar' education institutions have also stimulated interest in the so-called 'smart school' and 'sentient school'. These inferences of knowing and awareness reflect the idea of school as a place that consists of a combination of 'analogue' physical spaces and the 'digital' online spaces that are programmed and coded around them. This is not as far-fetched as it might sound. For instance, lessons taking place in physical classrooms now routinely involve activities conducted through data-driven 'learning management systems'. Conversely, school corridors, hallways and playgrounds are replete with CCTV systems, motion sensors, RFID tags and fingerprint biometric technologies to track the movement of people and resources through school environments. These are all instances of educational institutions taking the form of what Rob Kitchin and Martin Dodge describe as 'Code/Space', where software and systems are used in real-life spaces to support new activities, relationships and practices.[8]

This convergence of code and space is intensified if one considers the thousands of personal digital devices in the possession of the students and staff within a school. Again, data trails from these devices are being utilized for educational purposes. For example, physical education and health classes now make use of students' personal tracking and monitoring devices (such as fitness bands and smartphone apps) that collect data on sleeping behaviours, brain activity, diet, blood levels and heart rate as well as their physical movement.[9] In this way, schools are becoming what Ben Williamson has termed 'data platforms' where students and teachers are subject to continuous data tracking, sensing and monitoring. In theory, this all takes place with the aim of improving behaviour and performance: 'Data-tracking technologies are now being positioned to provide a constant stream of knowledge, in real time, about the activity and performance of every aspect of the institution, from facilities and administration to classroom pedagogy and student progress.'[10]

The benefits of data-based education

Data, analytics and algorithms play a central role in what contemporary 'education' is. They also represent the increased involvement of a range of actors and agendas in education. On one hand, data continue to be used by official authorities and agencies to provide new insights about systems and new means to govern and regulate. Data also continue to be used by schools, colleges and universities to provide insights into the effectiveness of institutional provision. Conversely, data also bring other groups to the forefront of education. Data are now used by parents, students, employers and other 'consumers' of education to draw their own conclusions and perhaps to challenge official agendas. More companies now offer commercial data services to education – collecting, managing and analysing educational data on behalf of schools or even individuals. Some companies are collecting education data for their own purposes, often through the use of their products, while other companies are selling education data to third parties.

This plurality of interests has prompted various claims and counter-claims over the educational significance of data, leading some commentators to herald data as 'the future of education'.[11] Many different arguments, agendas, actors and advocates have contributed to the increased prominence of 'data' in education. On one hand, the educational developments just described resonate with technologists and data scientists eager to import tools and techniques from emerging fields of computational science into real-world contexts such as schools and universities. The promises of data-driven economies of scale and accountability also chime with those seeking the business-like reform of school and university systems. From this perspective, data are an ideal means of bringing market values and free market mechanisms into otherwise closed public education settings. Yet data also appeal to the democratic sensibilities of so-called 'social entrepreneurs' and progressive educators, drawn to the ethics of the 'open' sharing, reuse and collective development of data along non-proprietary, 'free' lines. Data are an educational innovation that has broad appeal.

The potential educational changes associated with data are substantial. In terms of economic impact, for example, one report from McKinsey Global Institute reckoned that efficient use of data could lead to around $1 trillion in value being added to education every year. McKinsey argued that educational data represented 'substantial opportunities to increase the efficiency and effectiveness of current systems. By standardizing and sharing data that already exist, the effectiveness of education around the world could be greatly improved.'[12] The McKinsey report described data as relevant to five distinct areas of education improvement. These included learning analytics for 'improved instruction', using school performance data to help students to choose programmes better and using skills data to match students to employment opportunities more accurately. In addition, transparent financial data would allow students to make more informed choices of tertiary education on the basis of actual expected cost, while education institutions could also use market and demographic data to plan and procure resources better.

Some would judge this analysis as too conservative, arguing that data and analytics mark the end of traditional education systems altogether. As Viktor Mayer-Schönberger and Kenneth Cuiker contend, the power of data (and particularly big data) 'will fundamentally alter education'.[13] Specifically, data about learners and learning have been celebrated by such commentators as taking the decision-making power away from education institutions and educators. Companies such as Knewton pride themselves on being able to 'teach you almost any subject better and faster than a traditional class can'.[14] As such, education decisions and choices seem to be made on the basis of evidence rather than intuition and informed by involved individuals rather than detached institutions or professionals: 'By gathering and analyzing more information about how each of us learns, we'll be able to tailor the experience to the precise needs of individual students, a particular teacher, and a specific classroom. The nature of education fundamentally changes, because with big data, society can finally learn how to learn.'[15] Similar sentiments inform calls for the corporate reform of education. Data can be used to take educational decision-making away from the confines of experts and institutions and place it in the hands of individuals. As one *Forbes* commentator concluded when arguing for realigning the school curriculum along the behaviourist lines of B.F. Skinner's programmed instruction, 'The secret ingredient is to keep "educators" completely away from the project.'[16]

At the other end of the ideological spectrum are equally passionate calls for the use of so-called 'open data' provision and practices as a means of supporting equitable and empowering forms of public education. The notion of open data has developed within information and computer sciences over the past twenty years – advocating unrestricted access and use of 'publicly acquired' data for as many people as wish to use it.[17] In theory, then, open data applications and practices offer a chance to support radical realignment of education in terms of transparency, accountability, public participation, engagement and collaborative change. The potential educational benefits of open data – especially in schools, colleges and universities – are many. For example, proponents talk of the 'open innovation' that can take place through the sharing of data throughout all groups involved in an educational institution.[18] This includes the reconfiguration of organizational roles, rules and norms, and a general 'democratization' of decision-making towards the periphery of school and college communities.[19] Such open data practices have, for example, allowed campaigners to reconfigure publicly available data sets to highlight the strong correlation between perceptions of safety in New York schools and education attainment.[20] Elsewhere, open data tools have been used by parents in Philadelphia to monitor and contest the under-resourcing of school libraries.[21] Open data initiatives are therefore seen to support increased transparency and accountability within institutions, which in turn offer the potential for increased efficiency, productivity and social innovation.

The case against calculation

All of these examples illustrate the allure of data for educators and educationalists. Algorithms, analytics and data mining all carry the promise of bringing technical precision to what is otherwise an imprecise and unpredictable area of society. This allure of 'instrumental rationality'[22] is not unique to education. As Rob Kitchin notes, much of the recent excitement about big data analytics across business, government and science has been driven by the idea that data 'can provide the answer to all problems' where 'complex social solutions can be dissembled into neatly defined problems that can be solved or optimized through computation'.[23] These ideas chime with long-standing theories in fields such as cybernetics, artificial intelligence and 'machine learning' that seek to harness the power of mathematical modelling, statistical analysis, feedback and algorithms. These ideas also fit with the recent refocusing of education systems over the past thirty years around notions of measurement, evidence and outcomes – apparent in the greater emphasis placed on the use of targets, benchmarking, performance indicators, comparison and accountability.[24]

Yet it is precisely the imprecise, complex nature of education that informs the arguments *against* the growing use of data-based 'solutions' in education. Perhaps the main contention against an increasingly data-based education is the inherently reductive nature of these data-based processes. Every data system faces questions of validity: that is, does it measure what it purports to measure? Many aspects of education are *not* easily defined, quantified and captured. Fierce debates still rage as to whether it is possible (and if so, how) to measure 'intelligence'. If debates over IQ have persisted for more than one hundred years, how accurately can other aspects of education, such as attention, satisfaction, effectiveness or motivation, be quantified and captured? Digital data (and their analysis) are therefore more accurately described as a contestable process – 'often unreliable, prone to outages and losses'.[25] Questions need to be asked regarding the reductions implicit in how education is now 'known' through digital data. Often these reductions relate to the marginalization of 'soft' social factors at the expense of more easily represented 'hard' facts. Moreover, many data-based representations of education can be criticized for overlooking issues of historical context and connections with past events, as well as what could be termed 'a humane and moral sense of the academic endeavor'.[26]

The danger exists of educational data systems only measuring what can be easily measured, rather than what cannot be easily measured but is nevertheless important. Gert Biesta refers to this as 'normative validity': that is, 'the question whether we are indeed measuring what we value, or whether we are just measuring what we can easily measure and thus end up valuing what we [can] measure'.[27] As Evgeny Morozov contends, many algorithms and analytics are concerned primarily with informing predictive and anticipatory action, with little or no concern for 'wider' questions of causation, context or consequences.[28] The information gathered by and for data systems – and the actions then taken with this information – therefore tends to centre on operational concerns rather than nuance of social meaning.[29]

Data-based interventions can also be criticized for restricting the ways in which education is governed and controlled. Central to this are concerns over the role of digital data in reinforcing and intensifying cultures of managerialism within education. Clearly, data are now an integral element of managerialist techniques of accountability, auditing, 'evidence-based' practice, effectiveness, indicators, and so on. Students and teachers are accustomed to being judged by their 'data profiles', with data-driven decision-making often inevitably distanced from actual educational contexts. As Rob Kitchin puts it, data analysis can 'unmoor' analyses of educational problems from the social, cultural and political realities of what the data are supposed to represent.[30]

Such issues are certainly apparent in the rise of so-called 'dataveillance': that is, the monitoring and tracking of students and teachers as they engage in online learning and other forms of technology-based education. The downside of the use of data for 'learning analytics' and personalization is that teachers and students become increasingly aware of being tracked and watched, and then alter their behaviour accordingly. Behaviour can become 'self-governing' and 'self-regulated' – conforming to what people perceive to be the norm, and therefore diminishing the individuality or flexibility of educational engagement. Similarly, the automated surveillance and heightened visibility that are implicit in many online learning environments can engender forms of 'coded suspicion' between educators, administrators and students.[31] Effective teaching and learning are difficult to achieve, more so if participants feel that their every move is being monitored and measured.

Questions can also be raised over the reproduction of inequalities within education through digital data. One key concern relates to the reinforcement of imbalances in power and control through data-driven processes. Take, for instance, the unequal opportunities that different people are presented with when engaging with digital data. Put crudely, distinctions often appear between those who have data 'done to them' as opposed to those who have the ability to 'do data'. In this sense, Lev Manovich has warned of a hierarchy of 'data classes' associated with the increased use of digital data in society.[32] This ranges from a majority of individuals who simply create data for others to process (and are largely unconscious of doing so); those who create data but are often conscious of doing so; those who have the means to collect data; and finally those who have the expertise to analyse data. Clearly, these different groups are ordered along lines of technical and statistical expertise – what Manovich has described as a 'data analysis divide' between data experts and those with fewer computational skills.

These issues are certainly evident in how digital data are now being used throughout educational contexts. On one hand, cadres of data analysts, data managers and information officers are employed in schools, colleges and universities to deal with the processing and analysis of digital data. Data processing is increasingly experienced as institutionally driven and 'top-down' in nature. On the other hand, many students and teachers remain largely unaware of the extent of their daily production of data traces and trails. This raises the question of who is able to benefit in which ways from whose digital data in educational contexts. One study of the use of assessment data within US schools highlighted a stark disparity between classroom teachers (who tended to respond to data in a self-regulatory sense, i.e. seeing it as indicating changes required in their own practices) and school principals (who tended to see data primarily as indicating changes required in the work of others).[33]

Finally, data also raise a host of difficult questions over ethics and what could be seen as the 'human cost' of arranging education along such data-driven lines. One prominent concern is data privacy: that is, the right of individuals to control the visibility of their information flows across different data systems and information networks.[34] With the almost limitless sharing and distribution of data across digital networks, problems arise with respect to confidentiality as well as what is understood by 'public' and 'private' – particularly with regard to the traditionally collective nature of 'public' education. This has led to recent legislation in some US states requiring schools to ensure transparency concerning how their data are used and reused, brokered, and in some instances sold to third parties. A second tricky ethical question is how data relate to people's identities – especially how someone is determined and 'known' through the data on them that are collected and amalgamated. When it comes to considering issues of human rights and ethics, data are a complex presence in any education setting.

Conclusions

This chapter has considered the many ways that digital data are used as a means of organizing, measuring and rationalizing how education is provided and experienced. Data-based computations are a key means of monitoring and measuring how education is taking place, and reckoning what might be improved. For many people, data are seen as making education more calculable, and therefore programmable in terms of enabling them to compute solutions to educational problems.

The rising prominence of data, coding, algorithms and other programmable aspects of education is understandable, yet it needs to be treated as a cause for concern. As with technology in general,

'The act of data collection involves decisions being made about what "counts" and, it follows, what does not.'

this ambiguity relates to the fact that 'data' are not neutral. Admittedly, many of the examples discussed in this chapter relate to the measuring and analysis of procedural (and largely mundane) aspects of education. Yet the meanings that are attached to these measurements and analyses (alongside the decisions that then follow) are clearly subjective, biased, partial and compromised. Just because something appears 'automated' does not mean that it is objective, neutral and free from bias. The act of data collection involves decisions being made about what 'counts' and, it follows, what does not. The role of data in education is highly political in nature.

When reflecting on the issues and tensions emerging from this chapter, it helps to move beyond ideas of 'raw' data and data analysis as a dry, technical mathematical process. Data are not discovered in a raw form, but are produced through a sequence of deliberate decisions. Moreover, any analysis or algorithm is a finite series of decisions and judgements. Educational data are enmeshed with 'the ideas, techniques, technologies, people and contexts that produce, process, manage, analyze and store them'.[35] Thus when making sense of data and education, we need to acknowledge the values that underpin their implementation and use. Values, preconceptions and ideologies are present when an automated grading system 'decides' to fail a student assignment, or a learning analytic platform tweaks an instructional programme to suit an individual better. As Gert Biesta reasons, any form of education measurement involves values and value judgements:

> When we are engaged in decision making about the direction of education we are always and necessarily engaged in value judgments – judgments about what is educationally desirable. This implies that if we wish to say something about the direction of education we always need to complement factual information with views about what is desirable. We need, in other words, to evaluate the data and for this, as has been known for a long time in the field of educational evaluation, we need to engage with values.[36]

Data, coding and algorithms can clearly be of benefit for individuals and institutions involved in making education decisions and choices. When contextualized and taken as part of a wider perspective, data and coding can be a useful 'part of the story' of how education is conducted. Proponents of data-based decision-making in education would argue that there is a big difference between 'solving problems through coding' and 'solving problems then coding the solution'.[37] The danger, of course, lies in seeing data and coding as an absolute rather than relative source of guidance and support. Education is far too complex to be reduced solely to data analyses and algorithms. As with digital technologies in general, digital data do not offer a neat technical fix to educational dilemmas – no matter how compelling the output might be.

As such, there is little sense in judging the presence of data in education as a simple case of 'good' or 'bad'. Instead, we are perhaps better off seeing data systems, algorithms and analytics as 'various shades of grey' rather than a black-and-white issue. As Rob Kitchin concludes:

> It is not a case . . . that data are used simply in either good or bad ways; it is more complex than that. Often seemingly opposing outcomes are bound together so that people can be both liberated and coerced simultaneously – they gain personal benefit at the same time as they become enmeshed in a system that seeks to gain from their participation.[38]

FIVE

Making Education More Commercial?

Introduction

This chapter considers the argument that digital technology has proven a 'good' means of extending the
interests of business and commerce into education.
Of course, education has always had its commercial
aspects. Schooling in the 1700s and 1800s was provided largely through private fee-paying institutions.
Then, throughout the twentieth century, school systems
were influenced considerably by the multi-billion-dollar
textbook industry that grew up around them. Now,
however, digital technologies are extending the com-
mercialization of education into new realms. In short,
digital technologies have positioned the private sector
at the centre of how public education is funded, organized and delivered in ways that would have been hard to
imagine a few years ago.

In one sense, the commercial nature of digital
education is wholly understandable. Unlike many
other aspects of education, the ability to design,

develop, manufacture and implement digital technology is well beyond the capacity of national governments, official agencies or educators. Even though it constitutes a sizeable market for IT products and services, the education sector holds little sway over the production of digital technology. Put simply, commercial interests inevitably hold the upper hand when it comes to developing and producing the devices, software systems and applications that make up 'digital education'. Education therefore constitutes a major commercial market for technology.

This gives the private sector considerable leverage over the use of digital technologies in education. Indeed, commercial influences on digital education now take a variety of forms. For instance, corporations such as Microsoft, Apple and Google have extensive 'Education Divisions' dedicated to shaping how their products are used in educational settings. Other multinational corporations are also busy developing digital products and services for the education market. These range from publishing firms such as Pearson to toy manufacturers such as Lego, all keen to diversify their businesses away from traditional products and customer bases. Increasingly, digital education also attracts large-scale multinational corporations with little prior involvement in education. Rupert Murdoch's News Corporation, for example, has invested heavily in educational technology firms and services to the point of now marketing its own school-specific Amplify tablet computer. Conversely, at the lower end of the corporate food chain, education has become the focus for a thriving 'start-up' sector. Here, thousands of wannabe high-tech entrepreneurs with nascent 'ed-tech' ideas compete each year for funding from venture capital firms. All of these 'new' entrants into the education sector have their own particular ideas and agendas of what education could – and should – be.

This variety of enterprise reflects the fact that digital education is now very big business. One cautious estimate from the US Department of Education reckoned the global marketplace for education currently to exceed $5 trillion.[1] Within this ballpark figure, the market for higher education 'e-learning' products alone is worth $91 billion.[2] Similarly, sales of educational software and digital content to elementary and high schools in the United States neared $8 billion in 2011–12.[3] Venture capital investment in US ed-tech companies stood at $2.51 billion for the first half of 2015 – a figure that had already exceeded the whole of the previous record-breaking year.[4] In terms of corporate financing, a company producing maths and reading software – Renaissance Learning – was sold in 2014 for a record sum of $1.1 billion.[5] As such figures suggest, the shaping of digital education around the pursuit of profit is stronger than ever before.

The benefits of commercial involvement in digital education

Commercial involvement could be said to benefit digital education in a number of ways. First and foremost, the IT industry prides itself on its ability to design and develop new technologies that support efficiency and improvement in education. While the term is overused in the technology sector, the IT industry clearly meets the dictionary definition of 'innovation' in education: that is, introducing new products and ideas that support changes in the established way of doing things. Second, large transnational corporations enjoy economies of scale that dwarf public sector organizations. In particular, the resources of the largest technology corporations such as Google, Apple and Facebook far out-strip those of any education institution, organization or agency.[6] Private sector involvement in digital education also brings a heightened emphasis on quick results and demonstrable outcomes. After all, companies tend to be driven by their accountability to shareholders and stock markets. This leaves the IT industry confident in its ability to 'solve' the problems that have traditionally beset educational uses of technology. As one of Google's international Heads of Education put it: 'Technology was hard to deploy in schools and we're making the solutions we supply very easy to manage. . . . [N]ow technology is finally really able to work for schools.'[7]

These ambitions translate into a scale and speed of action and change not often experienced in the public sector. In short, these are organizations that thrive on 'thinking big' and acting quickly. Many people would contend that the private sector engenders an entrepreneurial spirit that is not often evident elsewhere in education. Regardless of their size and standing, most high-tech firms pride themselves on 'thinking differently'. Even the largest IT industry interests like to cultivate an 'outsider' and 'maverick' mentality. These companies see themselves as risk-takers and boundary-pushers, unfettered by establishment thinking or 'old money' business practices and traditions. This is certainly evident in the ed-tech start-up market, where fledgeling companies seek funding for what are sometimes niche and left-field ideas. While the large majority of these ventures quickly 'pivot' or fold altogether, every so often a speculative pitch will proceed into large-scale development. The hundreds of millions of dollars currently being invested in ed-tech start-up companies are driven by the logic of letting 'a hundred flowers bloom' in a way not usually tolerated in other areas of education.

All told, it is understandable that high-tech firms and entrepreneurs feel qualified to challenge and reform public education through the development of digital products and digitally driven practices. Digital technology and technology-driven business approaches certainly offer an alternative to the established status quo and the vested interests that some observers outside education suspect of impeding the emergence of 'twenty-first-century' education. It therefore makes sense that education stands its best chance of being 'fixed' through the outsider intervention and 'outside the box' innovation of commercial interests which can conjure the ingenuity and imagination that led to the development of Facebook, Google et al. As Sebastian Thrun (co-founder of online learning company Udacity Inc.) boldly reasoned: 'Education is broken. Face it . . . it is so broken at so many ends, it requires a little bit of Silicon Valley magic.'[8]

Digital education and the rise of 'Californian capitalism'

This evocation of 'Silicon Valley magic' merits closer scrutiny. What exactly is this 'magic', and why might it be associated so closely with a small region of Northern California? In fact, the idea of 'Silicon Valley magic' alludes neatly to the set of business practices and approaches that underpin the new high-tech economy and its increased interest in education. This mentality was detailed neatly by the British economist Will Hutton in a passionate account of a visit to Palo Alto during the early 2010s. After only a few days in the San Francisco Bay Area, Hutton wrote of his realization of the global significance of the strain of 'Californian capitalism' that characterizes Silicon Valley institutions such as Google, Oracle and even Stanford University. As he put it, we are increasingly living in a world where economics, politics, culture and society are being shaped by West Coast ideals of the power of computing, entrepreneurialism and a risk-taking approach to investment.[9]

The ways that Silicon Valley firms and their

followers look to do business, according to Hutton, are shaped profoundly by the programming and hacking backgrounds of their main protagonists. He argued that an ability to write computer code (and preferably a familiarity with university-level computer science) is now a prerequisite to any aspiring entrepreneur becoming wealthy and influential, let alone 'enabling something momentous to happen'. This logic is certainly borne out by the likes of Mark Zuckerberg, Larry Page, Sergey Brin, Larry Ellison, Peter Thiel, Jack Dorsey, et al. All of these high-tech billionaires remain steeped in a programmer mindset where a faith in computational power and an 'always on' networked way of life fuel a relentless focus on invention and innovation. This is a culture of all-night coding sessions and a succession of ambitious start-ups (most of which quickly fail), accompanied by a mass of similarly computer-savvy venture capitalists and 'angel investors' eager to take a punt on the next 'next big thing'.

While Californian capitalism is clearly motivated by an old-fashioned pursuit of profit, by framing its origins in cultures of coding and programming, Hutton saw it as driven by a distinctly new attitude towards doing business. These are ventures that are based on big ideas, solving computational problems, entrepreneurialism, openness, collaboration, learning through failure and relentless self-belief and optimism. Also evident is a necessary sense of precariousness and a need to keep moving and experimenting – most evident in the constant reinvestment of profits from past successes into new business propositions. This is a mindset that revels in the power of individuals rather than institutions, and the creative potential of manageable amounts of renewal and disruption.[10]

Perhaps most tellingly, Hutton's article picked up on the desire amongst many high-tech industry protagonists to 'make a difference' while also ensuring healthy returns for shareholders. Hutton enthused over Silicon Valley's 'nobility of intent' and value-driven desire to engage with 'immense' societal challenges such as world health and global poverty. Beneath the speculative investments and well-publicized stock market launches, his report from this supposedly new frontier also evoked a spirit of the counter-cultural hippie mentality that fuelled the 'home-brew' development of computing during the 1970s, '[where] successful entrepreneurship is about using frontier technologies to address human need and ambition. It understands it is part of society and owes a debt to the culture and public infrastructure that create it.'[11]

Thinking big, spending bigger – recognizing the extent of commercial influence on digital education

If we go along with this idea of 'Californian capitalism', then the turn towards education that many high-tech firms and technology entrepreneurs have recently taken makes good sense. Education is certainly an area of society where high-tech interests can be seen to 'make a difference' while also turning in a profit. This moves us beyond issues of education as a commercial market for technology, and into the more fundamental commercial reshaping of education. Thus while less high profile than its attempts to eradicate malaria or develop driverless cars, the involvement of the digital industry in education is understandably expanding. One obvious instance of this are the well-established and vast educational programmes run by all of the large multinational IT companies – often under the aegis of philanthropic programmes and 'corporate social responsibility'. These activities range from the physical design and construction of 'Schools of the Future'[12] to the development of teacher training programmes, alternative curricula and (of course) the provision of computer hardware, software and infrastructure to educational institutions.

Beyond such public-facing corporate programmes,

however, lie a range of far more ambitious and audacious interventions and initiatives in education also stemming from IT industry interests. Take, for example, the educational efforts made by Peter Thiel (founder of PayPal) through his 'Thiel Fellowship'. This involves young people being awarded $100,000 to drop out of college education and pursue their dreams by developing world-changing businesses rather than 'wasting their time at school and being burdened by incredible amounts of debt'.[13] Other entrepreneurial interventions in education have displayed even greater largesse. For example, one of Mark Zuckerberg's first personal projects outside of Facebook was 'Start-up: Education'. This non-profit foundation oversees a number of educational interventions, not least Zuckerberg's personal donations making good his promise to do 'something big' in education.[14] This has included donations of $100 million to the Newark school district and $120 million to schools in the San Francisco Bay Area. While only constituting a fraction of these school districts' billion dollar annual commitments, grand gestures of this sort are certainly not common in the otherwise under-funded world of public education.

These interventions illustrate clearly the power that the financial clout of the IT industry can wield in education. These are increasingly strong voices in conversations about education reform, setting the tone for how education is being imagined in the 'digital age' in a number of subtle (and often not so subtle) ways. Take, for example, the philanthropic efforts of Bill Gates, who has pursued a long-running interest in education reform since moving on from the day-to-day running of Microsoft. The Bill & Melinda Gates Foundation boasts an extensive educational programme. This includes the Gates Foundation's key role in driving recent US school reforms around standardized testing and the common core curriculum. Similarly, it has spent over $470 million on US higher education reform, commissioning research, funding projects and generally creating what the *Chronicle of Higher Education* called 'an echo chamber of like-minded ideas'.[15] As Diane Ravitch observed, 'It is difficult to find education organizations that have *not* been funded by the Gates Foundation.'[16] Throughout these efforts there has been a clear desire to reform public education around technology-driven innovation. According to Bill Gates: 'The education we're currently providing, or the way we're providing it, just isn't sustainable. Instead we have to ask, "How can we use technology as a tool to recreate the entire college experience?

How can we provide a better education to more people for less money?"[17]

Of course, the commercial grip on education and digital technology is not exercised solely through grand philanthropic gestures and high-profile foundations. We should not overlook the considerable 'soft power' of major high-tech corporations in education decision-making. Take, for example, the renewed interest in the teaching of coding and programming throughout elementary and high schools. The fact that so many people in education have recently come to see this as a 'good idea' resulted in no small part from sustained lobbying by what has been described as 'a who's who of tech industry elite'.[18] Thus much of the speech-making, funding of pilot programmes and behind-the-scenes appeals to government regarding the imperative to get coding into schools was driven (and continues to be driven) by key players from the computer games industry, internet firms and software developers as well as business employers and investors.

One especially active spokesperson in this coding push was the executive chairman of Google, Eric Schmidt. During the first few years of the 2010s, Schmidt made great efforts to get coding and computational skills onto the educational agenda of different countries. In what turned out to be a land-mark speech to the UK media industry, Schmidt advised emotively that 'your IT curriculum focuses on teaching how to use software, but gives no insight into how it's made. That is just throwing away your great computing heritage.'[19] Schmidt's advice, backed by powerful IT industry interests, has been used repeatedly by government ministers, education officials and administrators as evidence that 'something needs to be done'. When a powerful figure such as the head of Google deigns to take an interest in their education system, public officials have tended to take his pronouncements very seriously indeed.

As these activities suggest, corporate involvement in digital education is sometimes submerged in complex (and often tangled) networks of influence and power. This was evident, for example, in the rise to prominence during the 2010s of massive open online courses. The rapid growth of MOOCs was driven by the formation of three large 'spin-off' companies seeking to act as brokers for mass online university tuition. One of the largest of these was Coursera – a self-styled 'social entrepreneurial' for-profit company. While popularly perceived to be driven by a couple of Stanford professors, Coursera was bolstered by $85 million of venture capital funding. This investment came from the likes of Laureate Education Inc. (the investment arm of the World Bank), LearnCapital Venture Partners (with Pearson as their largest limited partner) and the powerful Russian venture capitalist Yuri Milner. Even in the case of MOOCs – usually celebrated for bringing free learning opportunities to the world's masses – digital education is distinctly commercial in its origins, intentions and sustenance.

In one way or another, commercial influences have a hand in most of the recent high-tech education reforms and initiatives. Indeed, if one takes time to 'follow the money', then high-tech firms are involved as supporters and promoters of most – if not all – recent educational technology developments and big ideas. This includes seemingly innocuous ideas such as 'digital badges', the 'flipped classroom', the 'gamification' of high school curricula or the concept of 'twenty-first-century skills'. All of these have been supported and sustained by the likes of Mozilla, the Gates and MacArthur foundations, Pearson, Cisco, Intel, Microsoft, Apple and a host of smaller IT corporate-associated names. Altogether, this industry activity is generating substantial pressure to reshape and redirect public education. In all these guises, then, the breadth and depth of commercial involvement in contemporary education reform should not be underestimated. As Kevin Carey observes, the biggest would-be movers and shakers in education are no longer educators or academics, but programmers, hackers and, of course, the trillion dollar industry that has grown up around them.[20]

Challenging the benefits of commercial involvement

The key question that now needs to be asked of everything so far covered in this chapter is 'So what?' So what does it mean that education is driven increasingly by technology-based commercial interests, ideas and investment? On the face of it, none of these commercially driven interventions into the world of education should be seen as especially problematic. Many people would consider it only proper that billionaire entrepreneurs plough some of their wealth back into needy communities. What is wrong with exploring technically efficient ways to make use of new technologies and techniques? Similarly, the conduct of these firms, foundations and their leaders is hardly out of the ordinary. After all, companies looking to make a profit are always going to act as efficiently as the market will allow them. Similarly, most businesses are accepting of the need to monetize seemingly 'free' products and services. None of the examples just outlined are particularly contentious ways of doing business with education and technology.

Yet many of these seemingly straightforward interventions have proven to be ineffectual and/or controversial. Despite the grand claims, most of the educational problems and crises being addressed through these corporate interventions continue to persist and perpetuate. In short, commercial reforms of education along digital lines have promised much but delivered far less. This highlights the problems implicit in the coming together of commercial interests, digital technologies and education. These problems are not necessarily caused by an educational establishment that is resistant to change and reform. Neither do they result from self-interested resistance amongst school districts, teaching unions or misguided parent groups. Rather than being instances of education 'not getting' the high-tech corporate world, many of the examples just outlined could be seen as instances where the high-tech industry has simply failed fully to 'get' education. Indeed, many of these problems could be said to stem largely from the private sector values that underpin much of what is blithely seen as the inevitable digital reform of public education.

In particular, innovations such as Coursera, Thiel Fellowships et al. could be seen as conforming to many of the core values of what was described earlier on in this chapter as Californian capitalism. All of these interventions convey a sense (at least implicitly) of 'education' being a discrete computational project: that is, a set of variables that can be manipulated and programmed in ways that avoid any 'bugs' or inefficiencies. As with most computational projects, there is a distinct preference for experimentation and learning through failure. As with many IT industry ventures, a great deal is expected to result from directing large sums of money towards specific problems. This knowing subversion of traditional business methods is coupled with traces of the emphasis placed within programming cultures on openness, the inefficiencies of institutions and 'experts', as well as a libertarian belief in the values of personal freedoms and the individualization of action.

All in all, this mindset makes for a markedly different approach to change and reform than is usually applied to education. To any education insider, ideas such as these are surely as terrifying as they might be thrilling. These are certainly different times for everyone involved in education. Indeed, given the novelty of such thinking, it is little wonder that commercially driven attempts to 'reboot' education have been welcomed in many circles. Ideas such as the MOOC and 'flipped classrooms' could well be seen as refreshingly imaginative attempts to move beyond inefficiencies and inequalities within public education systems. That said, there are certainly a few reasons for caution.

One obvious issue is an (in)compatibility of values and interests. While Bill Gates might like to talk of a 'virtuous cycle' between technology entrepreneurs and classroom teachers,[21] these relationships are not completely benign or altruistic. Any private sector involvement in public education takes place for a number of different reasons. These include the pursuit of profit, raising brand awareness and the 'up-skilling' of future workers. Whatever their specific motivations, firms and entrepreneurs are usually interested in imbuing education with different values and outcomes. A key question to consider is the extent to which these 'new' values and sensibilities are compatible with the traditional values and sensibilities of 'public' education.

In this sense, some values implicit in how the high-tech sector operates might not translate easily into education contexts. First and foremost is a potential misreckoning of the profitability of education markets and education consumers. Most of the forms of commercially driven 'change' and 'disruption' outlined in this chapter have been underpinned by lavish funding from outside of education in the (often unspecified) hope of future profitability or reward. Thus, much of what has been described in this chapter follows a model of financing that is familiar to the technology industry but largely unfamiliar to the education sector. As Audrey Watters observes:

> While education technology startups have become increasingly successful at landing (early stage) investment, the path to profitability hasn't been as clear. . . . It's a fairly common practice these days: release your [ed-tech] product for free. Gain users. Monetize later. If that doesn't work out, if you need more time to figure a business model out, simply raise more funding.[22]

Perhaps more fundamental than a lack of sustainable business models is a misreckoning of what commercial approaches are capable of achieving within education on the basis of previous successes outside of education. There is a tendency for high-tech

'There is a distinct naïvety – if not arrogance – in the ways that many commercial high-tech interests approach education change and reform.'

firms and entrepreneurs to rely on simply 'scaling up' models and approaches that have previously proved successful in commercial arenas. On one hand, this sees a privileging of big, audacious ideas and the ambitious application of business ethics to public settings. On the other hand, however, there is a lack of consideration for the contexts in which these ideas are to be enacted. Indeed, in his analysis of why none of the large ed-tech investments of the first 'dot.com' boom 'emerged as sustainable successes', Christopher Nyren pinpointed Silicon Valley's tendency to focus on 'shrink-wrapped' and 'over-engineered product' while ignoring the 'real market problems' faced by its education customers.[23] All told, there is a distinct naïvety – if not arrogance – in the ways that many commercial high-tech interests approach education change and reform.

Returning to concerns raised in the previous chapter, questions can also be asked of the commercial tendency to approach education as a system of variables that can be manipulated and modelled like a particularly complex computer-coding problem. This is inevitably a reductive approach to what is an obviously complex and chaotic social situation. For example, issues relating to social and moral relations are inevitably left out of any equation or algorithm

– however sophisticated – being used to model 'education' or 'learning'. These are not neat, bounded and quantifiable processes and systems. Education rarely contains variables that can be adjusted and recalibrated to achieve optimal cause and effect.

Furthermore, many of these commercial interventions are built around achieving success through multiple failures. This clearly is an efficient approach to high-tech business. For example, it is expected that the vast majority of start-up firms will fail while only a handful of 'game-changing' examples will eventually emerge. Yet this 'fail fast, fail often' approach does not necessarily translate easily over into gambling with the fortunes of school districts, schools or individual students. Such an approach certainly clashes with the traditional educational philosophy of supporting all learners to succeed. As a society, are we happy to treat education as an experiment that runs the risk of jeopardizing the life-chances of current learners in the hope of later eventual success? As Bill Gates reflected of his Foundation's forays into education reform, 'It would be great if our education stuff worked, but that we won't know for probably a decade.'[24]

Serious questions therefore need to be asked of the forms of 'education' being advanced under the banner of commercially driven 'innovation', 'disruption' and 'magic'. In particular, it could be argued that there are a number of public values that risk being lost within the brave new world of digital education reform. Take, for example, ideals of social cohesion, community, communal responsibility, collective good rather than individual gain. Also at risk are ideals of equality of opportunity and/or equality of outcomes. All told, we need to consider what is being lost – as well as what is being gained – in the rush towards the rearranging and reshaping of public education in the image of commercial high-tech interests, Silicon Valley entrepreneurs and their followers.

Finally, there is a need to question the extent to which commercial involvement might be undermining democratic processes of governance of education. The involvement and interest of major multinational, multi-billion-dollar companies clearly brings a touch of glamour and charisma to the otherwise dull backwaters of education administration and policy-making. High-tech firms and their leaders therefore play a large part in setting the agendas for contemporary education – especially when pointing out educational 'problems' and their attendant 'solutions'. Put simply, politicians and policy-makers will always be eager to listen when the likes of Bill Gates, Eric Schmidt, Mark Zuckerberg and colleagues have something to say on the subject of education. Yet the increased prominence of these interests in education reform comes at a cost. Digital education in countries such as the United States has become driven by what Anthony Picciano and Joel Spring termed a 'Swiss-cheese' style of government.[25] Put simply, it could be argued that state and federal authorities are incapable of regulating (or even keeping abreast of) what are now essentially 'privatized government services'. Instead, companies such as Google, Microsoft and their ilk can be seen as shadow education ministries – holding sway over what goes on within classrooms and schoolhouses, but with none of the accountability required of public officials.

Conclusions

Whether one agrees or not with the concerns laid out in this chapter, many of the 'new' forms of digital education being driven by commercial interests are based around decidedly different agendas and ideologies than we are used to encountering in public education. These shifts in tone and emphasis may, or may not, be a 'good thing'. Yet these are issues that require more recognition, debate and scrutiny from within the educational establishment. In particular, a number of difficult discussions need to take place. Do public education professionals want to be working with – or working against – these new forms of education? Are these reforms an either/or option, or can mutually beneficial compromises be reached? Do any plausible alternatives exist, and how might they be developed? Regardless of possible answers to such tricky questions, these reforms cannot be simply ignored or assumed to be insignificant or unthreatening. On the contrary, these commercially driven forms of digital education pose a significant challenge to the current public provision of education. This is something that all 'stakeholders' in education need to acknowledge and address as a matter of urgency.

SIX

'Good' Education and the Digital – So What Needs to Change?

Introduction

Regardless of how 'good' it is, technology is undoubtedly an integral aspect of contemporary education. With so many aspects of education now taking place with and/or through technology, it feels increasingly unnecessary to talk about 'digital education' or 'technology-based education' as distinct from 'education' in general. Yet, as this book has highlighted, the significance of recent digitizations of education lies in the potentially substantial changes and reforms that accompany them. The past five chapters have detailed some profound shifts in the ways in which education is beginning to be provided, arranged and engaged with. Digital technology is clearly reconfiguring the ways in which information and knowledge are created, accessed and used. It is undoubtedly altering the ways in which people communicate, interact and get together with others to learn. For better and worse, digital technology means that many of the cornerstones of education are altering rapidly.

Of course, these changes are not straightforward or unproblematic. This book has highlighted some of the recurring complexities of technology and education. One theme has been the large number of surface changes as opposed to few (if any) instances of genuine disruption of the status quo. The seemingly spectacular rises of MOOCs, learning analytics, adaptive testing and personalized learning networks have tended to obscure the continuation of long-standing educational inequalities, inefficiencies and inertias. This is not the first time such a conclusion has been reached. Critical commentaries of technology and education often begin with arch observations along the lines of *'plus ça change'*, 'old wine in new bottles', and so on. While the history of education and technology is more nuanced than such clichés imply, it is worth reminding ourselves that the digital innovation of the past forty years has not resulted in the reinvention of the many educational problems outlined at the beginning of this book. As the technology critic Neil Postman was often fond of concluding on this matter (borrowing from Henry David Thoreau): 'All our inventions are but improved means to an unimproved end.'[1]

What is 'good' anyway?

These observations of (un)improvement are all very well, but still leave the central premise of this book hanging: is technology *good* for education or not? Certainly the title of this book is a neat publishing device – a blunt but immediate way of unsettling cosy assumptions about technology and education. By raising the possibility that technology might *not* be a wholly good thing, the question 'Is technology good for education?' does an effective job of problematizing the topic from the very start. Yet this is clearly a weak basis from which to draw any suitably nuanced conclusions. Whether technology is good for education is not a clear-cut question with a clear-cut answer. The past five chapters should have convinced readers that it would be foolish to offer a simple 'Yes' or 'No' response. In drawing any conclusions, there first needs to be some agreement as to what is meant by 'good'.

In a philosophical sense, 'good' is usually taken to refer to some sense of importance and/or value. A topic such as technology therefore tends to be understood in terms of relative good rather than absolute good. There is no essential educational 'good' in digital technology. Instead, deciding on the 'good' of what has been covered in this book involves a set of value judgements – perhaps even moral judgements – over which there will inevitably be more disagreement than consensus. Everything from here on in needs to be seen as a matter of opinion and argument.

An immediate way of interpreting this book's titular question would be whether digital technology leads to 'effective' forms of education. In these terms, technology could be judged as at least partially 'good'. Certainly, much of the digital technology described in this book supports forms of education that are cost-effective for education providers and for education consumers. The economies of scale associated with digital technology are a major factor in its increasing implementation throughout education. Moreover, it is proving effective in terms of increasing the quantity and diversity of education that take place. That said, it would be unwise to see digital technology as *wholly* effective. For example, when 'effectiveness' first became an educational issue through the 'effective schools' movement in the 1960s and 1970s, it was framed primarily in terms of the ability of educators and institutions to educate students of all backgrounds, regardless of socio-economic status or family background. Looking back over the past five chapters, digital technology can certainly be accused of falling short on this front.

Thus any judgement on the educational 'good' of digital technology needs to extend far beyond numbers of courses and throughputs of students. As the philosopher Gert Biesta reasons, notions of 'effectiveness' (or similar favourite terms in educational circles such as 'excellence') are simply judgements about processes.[2] These labels say nothing about the outcomes of educational processes: that is, the content of education ('of what') or its aims and purposes ('for what'). Thus the criterion of 'effectiveness' is not a satisfactory way to understand a topic that is as societally important as education. Few people are willing, for example, to discuss topics such as GM crops or nuclear energy only in terms of whether they are 'effective' or not. We therefore need to think about what we consider *good* education to be in more detail. This is clearly not simply a value-free matter of 'effectiveness'. Instead, this is clearly a value-laden matter that relates to one's opinions and beliefs regarding the 'whys' and 'what fors' of education.

At this point, discussions about educational values often diverge along lines of being conservative or progressive, traditionalist or liberal. Yet these positions tend to reduce discussions about education to an unhelpful set of either/or propositions. While clearly value-driven, these positions often skirt around the fundamental question of what the aims and ends of education should be. In this sense, it is perhaps more useful to consider the 'good' (or not) of technology in more nuanced terms of what we believe 'education' to be for. In this sense, Biesta suggests that there are three main functions of education that digital education might be judged against:

- *'qualification'* – that is, giving individuals the knowledge, skills, understandings and dispositions that allow them to 'do something': this might be training for employment, but could also be civics, citizenship, contributing to culture or generally being able to function in society;
- *'socialization'* – what Biesta describes as 'insert[ing] individuals into existing ways of doing and being',[3] becoming members of particular social, cultural and political 'orders', the continuation of culture and tradition – in a desirable and undesirable way; and
- *'subjectification'* – giving individuals a sense of who they are, encouraging the ability to act autonomously and think independently and critically.

Judged in these terms, then, education is not only about individuals (or groups of individuals) being able to learn abstract concepts and skills. Education is also related to how people gain a sense of themselves and their place in the world. This raises the need to consider technology and education in terms of what could be described as social good, public good and/ or common good. These forms of 'good' relate to benefits that are shared amongst all (or at least most) members of society. This extends any judgements of the 'good' of technology for education beyond potential benefits to individuals and their personalized 'learning'. Instead, we need to also consider the benefits to society as a whole: that is, the extent to which digital education is acting in the best interests of everyone.

So to what extent can digital technology be said to be 'good' in these diverse terms? Clearly, digital technologies are supporting the development of *some* forms of knowledge, skills and understandings, but it could be argued that other forms are less prevalent. Similarly, to what extent is digital education giving *all* individuals a coherent and rounded sense of their place in the world, and a grounding in wider society, culture and politics? Questions can be raised regarding the widespread development of autonomous action, as well as independent and critical thought. It is clear that technology has its educational inefficiencies as well as efficiencies.

Technology and education – a digital diminishment?

Many of the apparently 'good' values of digital education described in this book centre on the freedoms, rights and interests of individuals. Underpinning much of what has been described is the implicit belief that education is best provided, accessed and consumed on a laissez-faire basis – with every individual free to choose what they wish 'anytime, anyplace, any pace'. Individuals are presumed to be autonomous and self-managing, and the free market is valued as an ideal means of supply and distribution. Digital education is generally conceived as an open economy – ideally to the point of there being no proprietary interests but always welcoming of the innovation and entrepreneurship of for-profit entities. These values are accompanied by a deliberate devaluing of institutional interests that are seen to exert a monopoly over these freedoms. As such, digital education is built upon a privileging of educational engagement that takes place on an informal basis: that is, education that is self-directed, unplanned and spontaneous rather than formally structured and provided by institutions and authorities.

These values have been a common feature throughout the development of information technology and digital culture over the past forty years – labelled variously as 'cyber-libertarianism',[4] 'techno-libertarianism'[5] and the 'stealth libertarianism of Silicon Valley'.[6] In their essay 'The Californian Ideology', Andy Cameron and Richard Barnbrook describe this as 'a mix of cybernetics, free market economics, and counter-culture libertarianism'.[7] As reasoned in chapter 5, these ideas have long held sway in the Silicon Valley model of technology development but are now increasingly coming to bear on mainstream business, industry and finance, as well as government and public sector services. In terms of education reform, this approach is manifest in an unquestionably forceful and aggressive approach towards tackling educational problems. As Haley Sweetland Edwards put it:

> This newer class of tech philanthropists . . . come to school reform having been steeped in the uniquely modern, libertarian, free-market Wild West of tech entrepreneurship – a world where data and innovation are king, disruption is a way of life, and the gridlock and rules of modern politics are regarded as a kind of kryptonite to how society ought to be.[8]

The forms of digital education described in this book resonate directly with shifts in economics and corporate thinking, especially 'neo-liberal' notions of the primacy of market forces, individual freedoms and the privatization of public sector monopolies. They also resonate with the reshaping of popular culture along digital lines, and a general rethinking of the role of large-scale public institutions in contemporary society. Yet while these might be seen as 'good' changes by some (particularly those outside of education), we must remain mindful of what is being sidelined (or even jettisoned altogether) when these values are applied to education and technology. These are subjective arguments to make, but they need to be made all the same. To borrow another riff from Neil Postman, the most important discussions that need to take place about digital education often are not questions of what technology will do but questions of what technology will undo.

From this perspective, digital technology could be said to be legitimating a 'hollowing out' of education along profoundly unjust and undesirable lines. This can be seen in a number of forms. First, there is the issue of denying individual differences. As has been discussed at various points in this book, many of the advances in technology and education tend to assume a norm of the 'universal learner' – someone who is self-motivated, well resourced, inherently sociable, altruistic, rich in time and good will, happy to experiment and able to fail with confidence. There is little consideration of differences between individuals and deviations from this norm – what sociologists might term 'the Other'. What is missing from a lot of digital education, therefore, is an empathy for – or a deep understanding of – the perspectives, predicaments and lives of others.

The ramifications of these shifts merit sustained thought and reflection. It is no good for well-educated, well-resourced and well-motivated proponents of technology and education to only see digital education from their own (privileged) point of view. Digital education needs to be considered from the position of multiple disadvantaged groups. Issues of class relations, economic dynamics and structures clearly underpin much of what has been discussed in this book. So do issues of gender, race, disability, sexuality, ability, nationality and citizenships. These are all fundamental factors in how societies (and the technologies within societies) operate. Moreover, all of these issues are inter-sectional and relational – all things that are rarely factored in to the digital education mix.

Second, there is the issue of obscuring inequalities of risk and responsibility. Digital education is undoubtedly a source of great rewards for some people, but with these rewards come far greater risks. What if someone does not make a good choice of education product or provider? What if someone engages in an educational pathway that is inappropriate for them, or not as suitable/taxing/empowering as other options might have been? Of course, every individual is theoretically free simply to stop and choose again. This notion of giving people the primary responsibility for managing risk will work well for some – what was identified in chapter 2 as the well-resourced, highly motivated, 'roaming autodidacts'.[9] Yet others might benefit greatly from the support, guidance and mentorship of those more knowledgeable: that is, educational experts. These sources of support are not always present and accessible in people's lives. Leaving everyone to their own devices is not the fairest or most just way of arranging educational participation.

Third, there is the issue of technology's role in marginalizing the collective and the commons. As with many aspects of education reform along 'neo-liberal' lines, digital education engenders what Michael Apple terms a 'desocializing sensibility', where matters of collective good and social justice are marginalized in favour of the presumed power of individual choice. In this sense, digital education

'Even the most committed and zealous proponent of digital education knows in their heart of hearts that nothing is going to be "fixed" through technology.'

opens a space for certain identities and closes down others. It gives people *one* option of who they are. They are *consumers*. They are to be motivated by one thing – individual gain based on one's choice of 'products'. Collective responsibility and an immediate concern for social justice, these things will take care of themselves.[10]

Of course, digital education is rarely seen as a totally solitary pursuit. Yet the forms of 'social' usually associated with digital education tend to involve temporary collections of individuals, rather than groups with common bonds and meaningful, lasting obligations. As Evgeny Morozov contends, through the rise of the digital society, 'we are losing the ability to talk about things at the level of the collective.'[11] As far as debates regarding digital education are concerned, this clearly relates to notions of collective politics, solidarity and collective action.

Finally, there is the notable dehumanization of the acts of learning and teaching that might be associated with digital education. As identified in chapter 4, current arrangements of digital education often have little to say with regard to individuals' relationships with others, and the social and political contexts in which they learn and act. There is clearly a need to bring the human element of 'education' into digital technology. Education should be something that is imbued with the 'labor of love, care and solidarity'.[12] In this sense, it could be argued, 'Efforts at transforming education that do not have as one of their aims the cherishing of these norms and values threaten what makes education different from simply training.'[13]

Doing things differently?

The relationship between technology and education is obviously complex. This is a reasonable and fairly common conclusion for any academic author to reach. Yet it not enough to conclude smugly that things are more complicated than they might appear, and then move on. As Steve Fuller argues, there is an 'inevitable uncertainty' to any area of society if one looks at it in any depth or detail.[14] Meanwhile, people outside of the academic social sciences are able to manage complexity and work around it reasonably well in order to carry on functioning. The value in an author stressing the 'complexity' of technology and education is in explaining exactly what things are complex; then explaining why these things are complex; and then highlighting important factors of this complexity that usually escape people's attention but might offer a way forward – or what Fuller terms 'some larger prospect'.

Hopefully, the book has unpacked what the complexities of technology and education are. The final question is the deceptively simple one of 'So what?' What can we do with this knowledge in order to work around the less 'good' aspects of digital education? What can be taken forward in order to function in a slightly more desirable way: that is, a manner that is more fair, socially just, humanistic, focused on common rather than individualized concerns, focused on the public good rather than private profit? In addressing these concerns, we do not want to descend into the retrogressive, conservative stance of being 'anti-technology' – arguing impotently that technology must somehow be taken out of education altogether. We cannot simply deny the existence of digital technology. We should not give up altogether on the potential of digital technology to support better forms of education. Instead, it should still be possible to offer alternatives *and* push back against the current ways of doing things.

At this point, our thoughts need to turn to how such trends might be challenged and possibly countered. This involves considering alternative forms of digital education that might be capable of retaining (and perhaps revitalizing) the ideals of public education. In particular, a number of possible solutions might be explored for 're-scripting' digital education as a site for sustained public debate and political controversy. Therefore, let us finish this book by at least attempting to come up with a few alternative ways of 'doing' technology and education.

Maintaining a sense of hope about technology and education is not an easy task. Even the most committed and zealous proponent of digital education knows in their heart of hearts that nothing is going to be 'fixed' through technology. As Bill Gates was recently driven to conclude, '[E]radicating malaria, tuberculosis and polio is easier than fixing the United States' education system.'[15] Yet there is merit in not dismissing technology and education as a completely hopeless case. Part of the spirit of being critical is 'a consistent belief that there must be better ways of doing things than are currently found in the world'.[16] In the case of technology and education, this relates to realigning digital education in ways that are more democratic and focused on the common good, human-facing, ethical and caring.

These are not easy things to achieve (otherwise they might well have been achieved by now). But we should conclude this book by at least imagining how they might be. In doing so, there is a need to not be ashamed of putting forward suggestions that might appear impractical, unrealistic or implausible. As Robert W. McChesney argues, in proposing ideas to make digital technology a 'radical force' for democracy, we need to 'demand the impossible . . . unless we can begin to imagine the impossible, it may never become realistic.'[17] This is perhaps a highly sensible approach to take. Here, then, are three impossible sets of suggestions for the future of technology and education.

The first of these unrealistic proposals would be *to make technology and education an area of extensive and intensive state involvement.* The present positioning of technology and education around laissez-faire models of individual choice, private profit and commercial interest is clearly not acting in the best interests of the majority of people. There is an obvious need for good governance of technology and education. In this respect, what is required is the presence of strong guiding forces that are tasked with acting in people's interests. This raises the need for public institutions that are digitally competent, confident and forward-looking. Rather than leaving it 'to the experts', the state should be one of the leading experts when it comes to education. To retreat from the digital reform of education is a dereliction of duty for any contemporary state. Of course, the state and public sector in any country are by no means perfect and there is a clear need for state institutions to be upgraded to be more transparent, accountable and democratic. There are also many countries around the world where the state is the antithesis of democratic values. Yet, rather than give up on the potential of state-directed education altogether in the digital age, this is precisely the right time to be reconstituting and re-educating the state to serve the population better.

Effective state governance of digital education would require public organizations and institutions that are highly focused on digital technologies and digital practices. These would be institutions that actually know, care and are confident about technology and education. State direction of technology innovation is not as fanciful as it sounds. State agencies and state financing have underpinned the development of technologies as diverse as supersonic passenger planes, the internet and every key technology that goes to make up a smartphone – from the touch screen to GPS. Now, the majority of the development of climate change technologies is being funded by state investment banks and driven by public sector organizations.[18] Why should this not also be the case with technology and education?

Second, there is the prospect of *curtailing the activities of commercial for-profit interests*, and mandating the ethical 'selling' of technology to education. Education needs to be seen as one area of society where it is not acceptable to engage in the speculative profiteering that runs rife throughout the commercial IT sector. If commercial interests are to be allowed free rein in the areas of a country's consumer electronics or business supply, then a reasonable trade-off could be that they treat public education 'customers' in that country as a special case. Efforts need to be made to ensure somehow that corporate interests act in ways that genuinely serve education – not the other way around.

One possible way forward in this respect is requiring IT companies to engage with education customers along different lines. There has been much talk in the aftermath of the late 2000s global financial crisis of 'corporate social responsibility', 'corporate citizens' and the emergence of the 'ethical corporation'. If 'corporate social responsibility' is genuinely about ethics and not only a profit-maximizing exercise, then technology and education should be considered a key area for commercial technology interests to prove their socially responsible credentials. As Emma Carragher puts it, 'Businesses exist through the coop-eration of society, so have obligations they must keep in order to be allowed to exist.'[19] This is not as far-fetched as it might sound. As suggested earlier, at the heart of the IT industry is a counter-cultural, hippie belief in technology as a force for progressive change. We need to rekindle this philosophy and reclaim the direction of technology development from the gadfly concerns of Silicon Valley thinking and ideologies. In this sense, corporate social responsibility in educa-tion and technology could take a number of different forms:

- simply giving technology devices and services away, or at the very least selling them to educators and edu-cation institutions at no more than cost price;
- offering ongoing support for technology use and implementation in education settings;
- bringing educators and educational concerns into the design and development processes of products that will be used by education consumers (e.g. develop-ing a word processor for primary schools rather than requiring primary schools to use software developed for the business sector); and

- engaging in the ethical production of education technology products: for example, the 'fair trade' sourcing of components and manufacturing of products, ensuring (outsourced) workforces are paid at levels exceeding a living wage.

Third, there is the need to *reconfigure the topic of technology and education as a site of controversy* – what Keri Facer calls a site of 'quality conservation' amongst all the publics involved in education.[20] There are pertinent examples of technology and society that match this brief, such as recent public debates about 'fracking', GM foods, climate change, and so on. These controversies have seen sustained debates in news media, popular culture and politics, leading to tangible changes in public policy and private sector practices. There are educational issues that have also reached similar levels of public engagement, such as recent push-backs in some countries against religion in schools and national testing regimes. One could even count the moderate success of the public campaigns against the quality of school meals by high-profile figures such as Jamie Oliver.

So, given its importance and apparently compromised nature, why should technology and education not be a similar site of public deliberation, debate and dissensus? There have been plenty of possible 'controversies' highlighted in this brief book that should be the focus for public anger and argument. Yet, for the most part, technology and education continue to be discussed in the same vacuous and superficial terms. Much of the discourse that surrounds digital education could be said to fit neatly with what Harry Frankfurt famously described in his 1986 essay 'On Bullshit'. This is language that does not set out deliberately to lie or hide the truth *per se*. It is, however, excessive, phony and generally 'repeat[ed] quite mindlessly and without any regard for how things really are'.[21] This indifference to the facts and realities of the situation being spoken about is one of the most concerning aspects of the malaise that surrounds technology and education. As Frankfurt reasoned, such bullshit is more dangerous than outright lying as it implies a cynical giving-up on being bothered if there is any truth or authenticity to a subject.

It is clear that the ways in which technology and education are talked about can be vastly improved. In short, we need to change the conversation about technology and education to focus accurately and honestly on matters that concern the majority, and seek to stimulate a better 'public understanding of technology and education'. This involves repositioning all students, educators and parents as the subjects (rather than the objects) of digital education. This involves giving otherwise marginalized voices an agentic role in determining and discussing what digital is, and what it should be. Bullshit only persists and pervades, Frankfurt reasoned, because too many people who know little about a subject feel impelled or required to talk about it. Encouraging more public conversations about digital education by those who are directly experiencing it can only be a good thing – offering an antidote to the unsubstantiated and uninformed nature of much current public discourse on the topic.

Such perspectives are clearly not getting the publicity they deserve. In contrast, this book has highlighted a fair number of speculative pronouncements and judgements on technology and education from high-profile voices who clearly do *not* know better. Well intentioned or not, there is no benefit in people like Newt Gingrich, Eric Schmitt, Bill Clinton and their ilk dominating the public conversation about technology and education. Unless these spokespeople have a sustained interest in digital education, then their half-baked sound bites should not be influencing what goes on. Instead, the conversation around technology and education needs to be a genuinely public one. We need to reverse the current situation where educators are confined to asking 'what works?' while only elite powerful interests get to decide 'what matters?'[22] Above all, this means that professionals and experts need to increase their efforts to engage in more thoughtful communication and engagement with popular media and other public arenas – being more honest about the uncertainties of the subject and refusing to pander to the desires of news media for a lazy sound bite about digital transformation or digital dystopia.[23]

Conclusions

This is a book that has presented much to agree and disagree with. While going somewhat against the grain, it has attempted to develop a tempered, measured and balanced prognosis of what continues to be an over-hyped and over-sold area of education. Books written about technology and education do not usually pay sustained attention to the social, political, economic and cultural complexities of the topic. So, having made the effort to cultivate these concerns and dissatisfactions, it is certainly worth continuing to engage with the 'bigger picture' of technology and education. There is much here for anyone concerned with the 'digital futures' of education to think over, talk about and (ultimately) act upon. Given the time, effort, resources and brainpower that have been dedicated to technology and education to date, it is surely worth raising our game and striving to establish this as a site of critically aware and genuinely insightful work.

So where should we go from here, and what might this work involve? For a start, there is an obvious need for continued discussion and debate about the conditions of technology use in education and what might be done to improve them. This will certainly require difficult conversations about where investments are most needed, and how efforts and resources can be best directed towards enhancing the life-chances of all individuals and the greater public good. This will also involve avoiding the familiar trap of assuming that technology will inevitably change education. Indeed, most of the 'ways forward' just outlined do not relate to how digital technology might make public education better, but how public education might make digital technology better. In some cases, perhaps the best conclusion is that making no use of technology is preferable to making some use of it. Other cases might simply require different uses of technology.

When it comes to technology and education, there is no 'one size fits all' solution.

As such, the main 'take-home message' of this book is the need for more proper 'grown-up' debates to take place around the complexities and contradictions of technology and education. If nothing else, the past six chapters have highlighted the need to think clearly and carefully about the *values* that we most want to underpin any use of technology in education. In this sense, most of the conclusions that have been drawn throughout this book relate to broader debates over educational equity, social justice and democracy. So perhaps it is most fitting to finish with a few value statements which readers are free either to take up or to argue against.

From what has been considered throughout this book, it would seem evident that technology and education can clearly do 'better'. To be more precise, technology and education could certainly be fairer than they currently are. So, in striving to make the best use of technology in education, surely we need to ensure that all forms of digital education are pursued primarily in the general interests of the public rather than the narrow interests of the well-resourced and the privileged few? Surely, technology and education is an area of contemporary society that needs to work in everyone's interests rather than being dominated by commerce, markets and profit? Surely, an over-riding concern for the collective rather than the individual is the only way in which technology can be reckoned honestly to be 'good' for education? These are the values that I would prefer to see hardwired into the digital futures of education – what about you?

Chapter 1 Digital Technology and Educational Change

1 *The Economist* (2014) 'Creative destruction', *The Economist*, 28 June (www.economist.com/news/leaders/21605906-cost-crisis-changing-labour-markets-and-new-technology-will-turn-old-institution-its).

2 Jeff Jarvis (2009) *What would Google do?* New York: Harper-Collins, p. 201.

3 Stephen Downes (2010) 'Deinstitutionalizing education', *Huffington Post*, 2 November (www.huffingtonpost.com/stephen-downes/deinstitutionalizing-educ_b_777132.html).

4 Martin Weller (2015) 'MOOCs and the Silicon Valley narrative', *Journal of Interactive Media in Education*, 1(5) (jime.open.ac.uk/jms/article/view/jime.am/558).

5 Martin Weller (2015)

6 DoSomething.org (2015) 'High school dropout rates' (www.dosomething.org/facts/11-facts-about-high-school-dropout-rates).

7 John Etchemendy (2013) 'Are our colleges and universities failing us?', *Higher Education Reporter*, 27 December (higheredreporter.carnegie.org/are-our-colleges-and-universities-failing-us/).

8 David Bromwich (2014) 'The hi-tech mess of higher education', *New York Review of Books*, 14 August (www.nybooks.com/articles/archives/2014/aug/14/hi-tech-mess-higher-education/).

9 Jeff Howe (2013) 'Clayton Christensen wants to transform

capitalism', *Wired*, 12 February (www.wired.com/2013/02/mf-clayton-christensen-wants-to-transform-capitalism/all/).

10 Michael Horn and Clayton Christensen (2013) 'Beyond the buzz, where are MOOCs *really* going?', *Wired*, 20 February (www.wired.com/2013/02/beyond-the-mooc-buzz-where-are-they-going-really/).

11 Todd Hixon (2014) 'Higher education is now ground zero for disruption', *Forbes*, 6 January (www.forbes.com/sites/toddhixon/2014/01/06/higher-education-is-now-ground-zero-for-disruption/).

12 Larry Cuban (1992) 'Computer meets classroom, classroom wins', *Education Week*, 13 February (www.edweek.org/ew/articles/1992/11/11/10cuban.h12.html).

13 Rudi Volti (1997) *Society and technological change* (second edition), New York: St Martin's Press.

14 Larry Cuban (1986) *Teachers and machines*, New York: Teachers College Press, p. 52.

15 Sonia Livingstone (2012) 'Critical reflections on the benefits of ICT in education', *Oxford Review of Education*, 38(1): 9–24.

Chapter 2 Making Education More Democratic?

1 Mike Dorning (1996) 'Clinton plan would put computer in every classroom', *Chicago Tribune*, 16 February (articles.chicagotribune.com/1996-02-16/news/9602160335_1_computer-school-district-christopher-columbus-school).

2 ABC News (2013) 'President Obama announces broadband-for-schools project at NC middle school', 6 June (abcnews.go.com/blogs/politics/2013/06/president-obama-announces-broadband-for-schools-project-at-nc-middle-school).

3 Bill & Melinda Gates Foundation (2009) 'Emerging technologies ready to reshape community colleges', press release, 3 December (www.gatesfoundation.org/Media-Center/Press-Releases/2009/

12/Emerging-Technologies-Ready-to-Reshape-Community-Colleges).

4 Paul Atkinson (2010) *Computer*, London: Reaktion, p. 159.

5 Tim Berners-Lee (2014) 'The web at 25: the past, present and future', *Wired*, 6 February (www.wired.co.uk/magazine/archive/2014/03/web-at-25/tim-berners-lee).

6 Kevin Carey (2015) *The end of college: creating the future of learning and the university of everywhere*, New York: Riverhead, p. 3.

7 Alison George (2013) 'Free online MIT courses are an education revolution', *New Scientist*, 219(2925): 29 (www.newscientist.com/article/mg21929250.300-free-online-mit-courses-are-an-education-revolution.html#.VC_QORYWFFI).

8 MIT Open Courseware (2015) 'The next decade of open sharing: reaching one billion minds' (ocw.mit.edu/about/next-decade/initiatives/).

9 John Watson, Larry Pape, Amy Murin, Butch Gemin and Lauren Vashaw (2014) *Keeping pace with K-12 digital learning*, Durango, CO: Evergreen Education Group (www.kpk12.com/wp-content/uploads/EEG_KP2014-fnl-lr.pdf).

10 Kevin Mooney (2011) 'Online charter school proponents envision the democratization of education', *The Pelican Post*, 24 August (www.thepelicanpost.org/2011/08/24/online-charter-school-proponents-envision-the-democratization-of-education/).

11 www.theschoolinthecloud.org/library/resources/the-school-in-the-cloud-story.

12 hellohub.org/.

13 one.laptop.org/about/mission.

14 Deborah Todd (2013) 'Technology education in Haiti becoming a priority despite disasters', *The Pittsburgh Post*, 20 October (www.post-gazette.com/news/world/2013/10/20/Technology-education-in-Haiti-becoming-a-priority-despite-disasters/stories/201310200267).

15 Aleks Krotoski (2014) 'Syria's children learn to code with Raspberry Pi', *Guardian*, 26 July (www.theguardian.com/technology/2014/jul/26/syria-children-learn-to-code-raspberry-pi).

16 Steve Kolowich (2014) 'Can you really teach a MOOC in a refugee camp?', *Chronicle of Higher Education*, 1 August (chronicle.com/blogs/wiredcampus/can-you-really-teach-a-mooc-in-a-refugee-camp/54191).

17 See, for example, Diether Beuermann, Julian Cristia, Santiago Cueto, Ofer Malamud and Yyannu Cruz-Aguayo (2015) 'One Laptop per Child at home: short-term impacts from a randomized experiment in Peru', *American Economic Journal: Applied Economics*, 7(2): 53–80.

18 Mark Warschauer (2003) *Technology and social inclusion: rethinking the digital divide*, Cambridge, MA: MIT Press, p. 2.

19 Nabeel Gillani and Rebecca Eynon (2014) 'Communication patterns in massively open online courses', *Internet and Higher Education* 23: 18–26. See also Jeffrey J. Selingo (2014), 'Demystifying the MOOC', *New York Times*, 29 October (www.nytimes.com/2014/11/02/education/edlife/demystifying-the-mooc.html?ref=education&_r=0_).

20 Rose Eveleth (2013) 'Online courses aren't actually democratizing education', *Smithsonian Magazine*, 22 November (www.smithsonianmag.com/smart-news/online-courses-arent-actually-democratizing-education-180947818).

21 See, for example, Katy Jordan (2014) 'Initial trends in enrolment and completion of Massive Open Online Courses', *International Review of Research in Open and Distance Learning*, 15(1) (www.irrodl.org/index.php/irrodl/article/view/1651); and Lori Breslow (2014), 'Studying learning in the worldwide classroom', *Research & Practice in Assessment*, 8: 13–25.

22 Patrick White and Neil Selwyn (2012) 'Learning online?

Educational internet use and participation in adult learning, 2002 to 2010', *Educational Review* 64(4): 451–69.

23 Tressie McMillan Cottom (2014) 'Democratizing ideologies and inequality regimes', Berkman Center for Internet & Society Series, Harvard University, Cambridge, MA (civic.mit.edu/blog/natematias/inequality-regimes-and-student-experience-in-online-learning-tressie-mcmillan-cottom).

24 Robert Merton (1968) 'The Matthew Effect in science', *Science*, 159(3810): 56–63.

25 Daniel Rigney (2010) *The Matthew Effect: how advantage begets further advantage*, New York: Columbia University Press.

26 Kentaro Toyama (2015*) Geek heresy: rescuing social change from the cult of technology,* New York: Perseus, p. 117.

27 Kathleen Lynch and John Baker (2005) 'Equality in education: an equality of condition perspective', *Theory and Research in Education* 3(2): 131–64.

28 Kalwant Bhopal and Farzana Shain (2014) 'Educational inclusion: towards a social justice agenda?', *British Journal of Sociology of Education*, 35(5): 645–9 (p. 645). Citing Raewyn Connell, 'Just education', *Journal of Education Policy*, 27(5): 681–3 (p. 681).

29 Douglas Kellner (2004) 'Technological transformation, multiple literacies, and the re-visioning of education', *E-Learning and Digital Media*, 1(1): 9–37 (p. 12).

Chapter 3 Making Education More Personalized?

1 Charles Leadbetter (2004) *Personalization through participation*, London: DEMOS (www.demos.co.uk/files/personalisationthroughparticipation.pdf?1266491309).

2 Nicolas Negroponte (1995) *Being digital*, New York: Alfred A. Knopf.

3 Catherine Needham (2011) *Personalizing public services: understanding the personalization narrative*, Bristol: Policy Press.

4 Hannah Green, Keri Facer, Tim Rudd, Patrick Dillon and Peter Humphreys (2006) *Personalisation and digital technologies*, Bristol: Futurelab, p. 3 (www2.futurelab.org.uk/resources/documents/opening_education/Personalisation_report.pdf).

5 AltSchool (2015) *Educational approach* (www.altschool.com/education#educational-approach).

6 Nichole Dobo (2015) 'Facebook founder and others invest $100 million in a private school model they hope can take root in the public system', *Hechinger Report*, 5 May (hechingerreport.org/facebook-founder-and-others-invest-100-million-in-a-private-school-model-they-hope-can-take-root-in-the-publicsystem/).

7 Annika Rensfeldt (2012) '(Information) technologies of the self: personalisation as a new mode of subjectivation and knowledge production', *E–Learning and Digital Media*, 9(4): 406–18.

8 Jeffrey Young (2015) 'Here comes Professor Everybody', *Chronicle of Higher Education*, 2 February (chronicle.com/article/Here-Comes-Professor-Everybody/151445/).

9 Anya Kamenetz (2010) 'How TED connects the idea-hungry elite', *Fast Company*, 1 September (www.fastcompany.com/1677383/how-ted-connects-idea-hungry-elite).

10 Dave White (2011) 'The learning black market', 30 September (tallblog.conted.ox.ac.uk/index.php/2011/09/30/the-learning-black-market/).

11 Dale Stephens (2013) *Hacking your education*, New York: Perigee, p. 9.

12 Daniel Greenstein and Vicki Phillips (2014) 'Five things you should know about personalized learning', *Impatient Optimists* (Bill & Melinda Gates Foundation), 15 November (www.impatientoptimists.org/Posts/2014/11/5-Things-You-Should-Know-About-Personalized-Learning).

13 Newt Gingrich (2014) 'Get schools out of the 1890s', *CNN*, 1 August (edition.cnn.com/2014/08/01/opinion/gingrich-schools-blended-teaching-technology).

14 Carl Rogers, cited in Richard Gross (1992) *Psychology: the science of mind and behaviour*, London: Hodder & Stoughton, p. 905.

15 Barry Zimmerman (2011) 'Barry Zimmerman discusses self-regulated learning processes', *ScienceWatch*, December (archive.sciencewatch.com/dr/erf/2011/11decerf/11decerfZimm/).

16 Lee Rainie and Barry Wellman (2012) *Networked*, Cambridge, MA: MIT Press (back cover).

17 Annika Rensfeldt (2012).

18 Jodi Dean (2014) 'Big data: accumulation and enclosure', p. 18 (www.academia.edu/7125387/Big_data_accumulation_and_enclosure).

19 Michael Young and Johan Muller (2010) 'Three educational scenarios for the future: lessons from the sociology of knowledge', *European Journal of Education*, 45(1): 11–27 (p. 16).

20 Daniel Schwartz and John Bransford (1998) 'A time for telling', *Cognition and Instruction*, 16(4): 475–522.

21 Vicky Duckworth and Matthew Cochrane (2012) 'Spoilt for choice, spoilt by choice: long-term consequences of limitations imposed by social background', *Education+Training*, 54(7): 579–91 (p. 589).

22 Zygmunt Bauman (2013) *Does the richness of the few benefit us all?* Cambridge: Polity, p. 24.

23 Tressie McMillan Cottom (2014).

24 Zygmunt Bauman (2013), p. 49.

Chapter 4 Making Education More Calculable?

1 Doug Laney (2001) '3D data management: controlling data volume, velocity and variety', Stamford, CT: META Group (blogs.gartner.com/doug-laney/files/2012/01/ad949-3D-Data-

Management-Controlling-Data-Volume-Velocity-and-Variety.
pdf).

2 Farhad Manjoo (2014) 'Grading teachers, with data from class',
New York Times, 3 September (www.nytimes.com/2014/09/04/
technology/students-grade-teachers-and-a-start-up-harnesses-the-
data.html).

3 George Siemens, Dragan Gasevic, Caroline Haythornthwaite,
Shane Dawson, Simon Buckingham Shum, Rebecca Ferguson,
Erik Duval, Katrien Verbert and Ryan Baker (2011) 'Open learn-
ing analytics: an integrated & modularized platform', Society
for Learning Analytics Research, p. 4 (solaresearch.org/Open
LearningAnalytics.pdf).

4 George Siemens et al. (2011).

5 Viktor Mayer-Schönberger and Kenneth Cuiker (2014) *Learning
with big data: the future of education*, New York: Houghton Mifflin
Harcourt.

6 Sal Khan, quoted in Stephanie Simon (2014) 'The big biz of
spying on little kids', *Politico*, 15 May (www.politico.com/story/
2014/05/data-mining-your-children-106676.html).

7 Jill Barshay (2013) 'Q&A with Knewton's David Kuntz: "Better
and faster" learning than a traditional class?', *Hechinger Report*, 1
July (hechingerreport.org/qa-with-knewtons-david-kuntz-maker-
of-algorithms-that-replace-teachers/).

8 Rob Kitchin and Martin Dodge (2012) *Code/Space*, Cambridge,
MA: MIT Press.

9 Deborah Lupton (2015) 'Data assemblages, sentient schools and
digitised health and physical education', *Sport, Education and
Society*, 20(1): 122–32.

10 Ben Williamson (2015) 'Algorithmic skin: health-tracking technologies, personal analytics and the bio-pedagogies of digitized
health and physical education', *Sport, Education and Society*, 20(1):
133–51 (p. 134).

11 Viktor Mayer-Schönberger and Kenneth Cukier (2014) *Learning with big data: the future of education* (Kindle-only edition), New York: Houghton Mifflin Harcourt.

12 James Manyika, Michael Chui, Diana Farrell, Steve van Kuiken, Peter Groves and Elizabeth Doshi (2013) *Open data: unlocking innovation and performance with liquid information*, McKinsey Global Institute Report (www.mckinsey.com/insights/business_technology/open_data_unlocking_innovation_and_performance_with_liquid_information).

13 Viktor Mayer-Schönberger and Kenneth Cuiker (2014), n.p.

14 David Kuntz quoted in Jill Barshay (2013).

15 Viktor Mayer-Schönberger and Kenneth Cuiker (2014), n.p.

16 Phil DeMuth (2014) 'How B.F. Skinner will save online education', *Forbes*, 15 October (www.forbes.com/sites/phildemuth/2014/10/15/how-b-f-skinner-will-save-online-education/).

17 Michael Gurstein (2011) 'Open data: empowering the empowered or effective data use for everyone?', *First Monday*, 16(2–7) (firstmonday.org/article/view/3316/2764).

18 Kevin Boudreau (2010) 'Open platform strategies and innovation: granting access vs devolving control', *Management Science*, 56(10): 1849–72.

19 Youngjin Yoo, Richard Boland, Kalle Lyytinen and Ann Majchrzak (2012) 'Organizing for innovation in the digitized world', *Organization Science*, 23(5): 1398–1408.

20 Ben Wellington (2015) 'Safe hallways, successful tests', *Data Science for Social Good*, 20 March (dssg.io/2015/03/20/import-ben-wellington.html).

21 The 'Stacked Up' campaign run by Meredith Brossard, Pam Selle and Jeff Frankl (www.stackedup.org).

22 Shannon Mattern (2013) 'Methodolatry and the art of measure: the new wave of urban data science', *Places*, November (places-journal.org/article/methodolatry-and-the-art-of-measure/).

23 Rob Kitchin (2014) *The data revolution: big data, open data, data infrastructures and their consequences*, London: Sage, p. 181.

24 Sam Sellar (2015) 'A feel for numbers: affect, data and education policy', *Critical Studies in Education*, 56(1): 131–46.

25 Danah Boyd and Kate Crawford (2012) 'Critical questions for big data', *Information, Communication & Society*, 15(5): 662–79 (p. 668).

26 Liz Browne and Steve Rayner (2015) 'Managing leadership in university reform: data-led decision-making, the cost of learning and déjà vu?', *Educational Management Administration & Leadership* 43(2): 290–307 (p. 304).

27 Gert Biesta (2009) 'Good education in an age of measurement: on the need to reconnect with the question of purpose in education', *Educational Assessment, Evaluation and Accountability*, 21(1): 33–46 (p. 35).

28 Evgeny Morozov (2014) 'The planning machine', *The New Yorker*, 13 October (www.newyorker.com/magazine/2014/10/13/planning-machine).

29 Scott Lash (2002) *Critique as information*, London: Sage.

30 Rob Kitchin (2014).

31 Dan Knox (2010) 'Spies in the house of learning: a typology of surveillance in online learning environments', paper presented to 'EDGE 2010: e-Learning: the horizon and beyond' conference, Memorial University of Newfoundland, Canada, October.

32 Lev Manovich (2011) 'Trending: the promises and the challenges of big social data', in Matthew Gold (ed.), *Debates in the digital humanities*, Minneapolis: University of Minnesota Press, pp. 460–75.

33 Matthew Militello, Lisa Bass, Karen Jackson and Yuling Wang (2013) 'How data are used and misused in schools', *Education Sciences*, 3(2): 98–120.

34 Neil M. Richards and Jonathan H. King (2014) 'Big data ethics',

Wake Forest Law Review, 19 May (papers.ssrn.com/sol3/papers.
cfm?abstract_id=2384174).

35 Rob Kitchin (2014), p. 185.

36 Gert Biesta (2009), p. 35.

37 Lisa Loop (2014) @LisaLoopED, 26 August (twitter.com/
LizaLoopED/status/504351036757524480).

38 Rob Kitchin (2014), p. 164.

Chapter 5 Making Education More Commercial?

1 Jordan Shapiro (2013) 'Grab a share of education's $6 tril-
lion marketplace', *Forbes*, 11 September (www.forbes.com/sites/
jordanshapiro/2013/09/11/grab-a-share-of-educations-6-trillion-
marketplace).

2 Audrey Watters (2013) 'The business of ed-tech', *Hack Education*,
23   December   (hackeducation.com/2013/12/23/top-ed-tech-
trends-2013-business).

3 David Nagel (2014) 'US PreK-12 is a $7.9 billion software
market', *THE Journal*, 8 January (thejournal.com/articles/2014/
01/08/siia-u.s.-prek12-is-a-7.9-billion-software-market.aspx).

4 Carl Straumsheim (2105) 'Ed tech's funding frenzy', *Inside
Higher Ed*, 24 July (www.insidehighered.com/news/2015/07/24/
investments-ed-tech-companies-reach-new-high-first-half-2015).

5 Michelle Molnar (2014) 'Billion-dollar deal heats up ed-tech
market', *Education Week*, 26 March (www.edweek.org/ew/arti
cles/2014/03/26/26acquisition.h33.html).

6 In 2014, Google was reinstated as the 'most valuable global
brand', with a valuation of $159 billion. The company that it
regained top billing from was Apple, with a brand value of $148
billion. In contrast, the GDP of New Zealand is in the region of
$122 billion. See Sarah Gordon (2014) 'Global brands: Google
pips Apple in popularity', *Financial Times*, 21 May (www.

ft.com/intl/cms/s/2/d8ea4e6e-da79-11e3-a448-00144feabdc0. html#axzz32O1tw2ZQ).

7 Liz Sproat (Google's Head of Education across Europe, the Middle East and Africa) cited in Matt Warman (2015) 'How Google is trying to muscle into Britain's schools', *The Telegraph*, 22 February (www.telegraph.co.uk/technology/11428123/How-Google-is-trying-to-muscle-into-Britains-schools.html).

8 Lisa Wolfson (2013) 'Venture capital needed for "broken" US education, Thrun says', *Business Week*, 18 June (http://www. bloomberg.com/news/articles/2013-06-18/venture-capital-needed-for-broken-u-s-education-thrun-says).

9 Will Hutton (2013) 'In California, I saw the virtues – and vices – of the new economy', *Guardian*, 14 September (www. theguardian.com/commentisfree/2013/sep/14/californian-capital ism-can-teach-britain).

10 See also Audrey Watters (2015) 'Ed-tech and the Californian ideology', *Hack Education*, 17 May (hackeducation.com/2015/05/17/ed-tech-ideology/).

11 Will Hutton (2013).

12 sof.philasd.org/about.

13 Vivek Wadhwa (2013) 'Billionaire's failed education experi-ment proves there's no shortcut to success', *Forbes*, 11 September (www.forbes.com/sites/singularity/2013/09/11/peter-thiel-prom ised-flying-cars-instead-we-got-caffeine-spray).

14 Dale Russakoff (2014) 'Schooled', *The New Yorker*, 19 May (www.newyorker.com/reporting/2014/05/19/140519fa_fact_russakoff?currentPage=all).

15 Marc Parry, Katy Field and Beckie Supiano (2013) 'The Gates effect', *Chronicle of Higher Education*, 14 July (www.chronicle. com/article/The-Gates-Effect/140323).

16 Diane Ravitch (2013) *Reign of error* (Kindle edition), New York: Knopf, n.p.

17 Marc Parry et al. (2013).

18 Kristen V. Brown (2014) 'Tech leaders lobby for coding classes in California schools', *SFGate*, 6 May (www.sfgate.com/technology/ article/Tech-leaders-lobby-for-coding-classes-in-5458627.php).

19 Torin Douglas (2011) 'Google's Eric Schmidt criticises education in the UK', *BBC News*, 26 August (www.bbc.com/news/ uk-14683133).

20 Kevin Carey (2012) 'The siege of academe', *Washington Monthly*, September/October   (www.washingtonmonthly.com/magazine/ septemberoctober_2012/features/_its_three_oclock_in039373. php?page=all#).

21 Benjamin Herold (2013) 'Bill Gates on teaching, ed tech, and philanthropy', *Education Week*, 16 August (blogs.edweek.org/ edweek/DigitalEducation/2013/08/qa_bill_gates_teaching_ edtech_philanthropy.html).

22 Audrey Watters (2013).

23 Christopher Nyren (2014) 'Why Silicon Valley sucks at EdTech', *Medium.com*, 16 June (medium.com/@EdTech/why-silicon-valley- sucks-at-edtech-aeee24d758da).

24 Valerie Strauss (2013) 'Bill Gates: "It would be great if our educa- tion stuff worked but . . .'", *The Washington Post*, 27 September (www.washingtonpost.com/blogs/answer-sheet/wp/2013/09/ 27/bill-gates-it-would-be-great-if-our-education-stuff-worked- but/).

25 Anthony Picciano and Joel Spring (2013) *The great American education-industrial complex*, New York: Routledge.

Chapter 6 'Good' Education and the Digital – So What Needs to Change?

 1 Neil Postman (1990) 'Informing ourselves to death', speech to the German Informatics Society (Gesellschaft für Informatik)

October, Stuttgart (w2.eff.org/Net_culture/Criticisms/informing_ourselves_to_death.paper).

2 Gert Biesta (2009).

3 Gert Biesta (2009), p. 40.

4 Langdon Winner (1997) 'Cyberlibertarian myths and the prospects for community' (homepages.rpi.edu/~winner/cyberlib2.html).

5 Clyde Wayne Crews Jr (2014) 'Techno-libertarianism: building the case for separation of technology and state', *Forbes*, 17 July (www.forbes.com/sites/waynecrews/2014/07/17/techno-libertarianism-building-the-case-for-separation-of-technology-and-state/).

6 Andrew Leonard (2014) 'Tech's toxic political culture: the stealth libertarianism of Silicon Valley bigwigs', *Salon*, 6 June (www.salon.com/2014/06/06/techs_toxic_political_culture_the_stealth_libertarianism_of_silicon_valley_bigwigs/).

7 Andy Cameron and Richard Barnbrook (1995) 'The Californian ideology', *Mute* 3 (www.hrc.wmin.ac.uk/theory-californianideology-mute.html).

8 Haley Sweetland Edwards (2014) 'The war on teacher tenure', *Time*, 30 October (time.com/3533556/the-war-on-teacher-tenure/).

9 Tressie McMillan Cottom (2014).

10 Michael Apple (2013) *Can education change society?*, London: Routledge, pp. 7–8.

11 Evgeny Morozov (2014) 'Against solutionism', keynote speech to DLD14 conference, Munich, January (t.co/977jkRRcHi).

12 Michael Apple (2013), p. 15.

13 Michael Apple (2013), p. 15.

14 Steve Fuller (2014) 'Sociology as the science of human uplift', keynote speech to the British Sociological Association Conference, April 2014 (vimeo.com/103788571).

15 Jeir Clausing (2014) 'Gates says fixing education biggest challenge',

Huffington Post, 1 July (www.huffingtonpost.com/2014/07/01/bill-gates-education-challenge_n_5547848.html).

16 Ash Amin and Nigel Thrift (2005) 'What's left? Just the future', *Antipode*, 37: 220–338 (p. 221).

17 Robert W. McChesney (2014) 'Be realistic, demand the impossible: three radically democratic internet policies', *Critical Studies in Media Communication*, 31(2): 92–9 (p. 93).

18 Paul Mason (2014) 'From Concorde to the iPhone, state intervention drives technological innovation', *Guardian*, 27 July (www.theguardian.com/commentisfree/2014/jul/27/concorde-iphone-history-state-intervention-technological-innovation).

19 Emma Carragher (2014) 'Are corporate social responsibility policies an indication of the rise of the "ethical corporation" or are they simply a public relations strategy?', *The SOCSI Review*, 1: 15.

20 Keri Facer (2011) *Learning futures*, London: Routledge.

21 Harry Frankfurt (1986) 'On bullshit', *Raritan Quarterly Review*, 6(2): n.p. (www.stoa.org.uk/topics/bullshit/pdf/on-bullshit.pdf).

22 Howard Stevenson (2014) 'Why teachers should be sceptical of a new College of Teaching', *The Conversation*, 16 December (theconversation.com/why-teachers-should-be-sceptical-of-a-new-college-of-teaching-35280).

23 See 'The perils of public debate', editorial in *Nature Neuroscience*, 8: 535 (www.nature.com/neuro/journal/v8/n5/full/nn0505-535.html).

access to education 16, 17, 27, 30, 31–3, 34, 37, 39, 44, 48, 50–2, 140
algorithms 56, 81, 83, 85, 91, 96, 98, 102, 104, 105, 106
Amazon.com 56
analytics 84, 85, 86–8, 93, 96, 98, 99, 105, 128–9, 134
Apple 54, 108, 110, 121

Berners-Lee, Tim 30
Biesta, Gert 98, 105, 137–8
big data 82, 88, 93–4, 96
Bill & Melinda Gates Foundation 26, 66, 118
'broken' education system 8–9, 11–13, 112
bullshit 155–156
business model 9, 18, 126

Californian capitalism/ Californian ideology 113–14, 116, 124, 141
change 5–8, 19, 20, 22–3, 30, 57, 92, 133–4, 142, 154, 155, 158

Christensen, Clay 15–17
Clinton, Bill 26, 156
coding 41, 81, 83, 102, 105–6, 114, 119, 128
computerized grading 84, 85, 105
corporate interests/values 21, 94, 109–10, 120, 123, 142, 152
corporate social responsibility 116, 152–3
Cottom, Tressie McMillan 45, 76
Coursera 35, 67, 120, 124
Cuban, Larry 19, 22
customization 54–7, 61, 72

disruptive innovation 15–17, 20

equality 48, 50, 51, 52, 130
equity 26, 40, 48, 50, 52, 159

Facebook 67, 110, 112, 117
fix (digital/technical) 8–9, 12, 15, 18, 21, 22, 24, 106, 112, 149

Index

Gates, Bill 118, 125, 129, 131,
  149
  see also Bill & Melinda Gates
  Foundation
Gingrich, Newt 66, 67, 80, 156
Google 1, 5, 61, 108, 110, 111,
  112, 113, 119, 120, 131

Hole in the Wall 38, 39, 41,
  43

individualism 69, 71
inequality 28, 30, 31–2, 45, 46,
  49, 50–2, 53, 75, 99, 125,
  134, 143
innovation 9, 15–17, 19, 20,
  21, 89, 92, 95, 110, 112,
  114, 118, 124, 130, 134,
  140, 141, 151
  see also disruptive innovation

Kitchin, Rob 90, 96, 99,
  106
Knewton 88–9, 93
knowledge 1, 2, 33, 61, 67, 73,
  74, 90, 133, 138, 139

libertarianism 12, 50, 70, 124,
  141

market (forces/values) 8, 10, 12,
  16, 17, 20, 22, 45, 50, 70,
  74, 76, 79, 92, 108, 116,
  122, 126, 140, 141,142,
  160

Matthew Effect 46, 50
Microsoft 54, 108, 118, 121, 131
Mitra, Sugata 38, 41
MOOCs 35–6, 41–4, 45, 64,
  76, 85, 120, 121, 125,
  134
Morozov, Evgeny 98, 146

neoliberalism 70, 142, 144
Netflix 67, 80

Obama, Barack 26
OLPC (One Laptop Per Child)
  39–40, 42, 43
openness 30, 35–6, 92, 94–5,
  120, 124, 140, 146

Pearson 88, 108, 121
Postman, Neil 134, 142
power 7, 11, 50, 53, 93, 100,
  119, 120, 144, 157
public good 139, 148, 158
public sector 8, 110, 111, 141,
  142, 151–2

Schmidt, Eric 119, 120, 131, 156
smartphone 1, 34, 54, 55, 90,
  151
start-up 17, 109, 111, 112, 114,
  129
state/government 2, 7, 11, 55,
  57, 71, 82, 84, 119, 131,
  150–2

Thiel, Peter 114, 117, 124

Index

university 7, 10, 11, 14, 18, 27,
   32, 35–7, 41, 64, 65, 92,
   108, 120

values 8, 16, 17, 20, 21–2, 24,
   51, 67, 79–80, 104–5,
   123–5, 130, 137, 140,
   142, 147, 151

venture capital 109, 114,
   120–1

Wikipedia 1, 17, 46
Williamson, Ben 90

Zuckerberg, Mark 61, 114, 117,
   131